Way With Worlds
Book 1: Crafting Great
Fictional Settings
(First Edition)

By Steven Savage

D1557416

Way With Worlds
Book 1: Crafting Great Fictional Settings

First Edition

ISBN-10: 1533164797
ISBN-13: 978-1533164797
Copyright © 2016 by Steven Savage

AUTHOR: Steven Savage
www.StevenSavage.com

EDITOR: Jessica Hardy

COVER ARTIST: Richelle Rueda
www.FireCatRich.com

First Edition

www.InformoTron.com

Acknowledgments

To all the readers of the original "Way With Worlds" columns who told me what they meant to them and made me realize it was time to rewrite them.

To all the users of Seventh Sanctum who inspired me to do this again.

To Serdar, Scott, Bonnie, Ewen, Jason, Paul, Carlos, Rob, Grant, and the rest of the gang for their support and feedback.

Thanks to my pre-readers:
- Gina Williams of **squeezleprime.tumblr.com** for all her notes!
- Duane Walton, who gave me a well-needed thumbs up. Her group, **www.facebook.com/groups/writeonminooka/**, is lucky to have her!
- Jackie Speel for her enthusiastic feedback!

Other Books By Steven Savage

Fan To Pro: Leveling Up Your Career Through Your Hobbies

Convention Career Connection

The Power Of Creative Paths

Activities For The Civic Geek

The Focused Fandom Series
- *Focused Fandom: Cosplay, Costuming, And Careers*
- *Focused Fandom: Fanart, Fanartists, and Careers*

The Career Series
- *Epic Resume Go!*
- *Quest For Employment*
- *Resume Plus*
- *Skill Portability*

Table of Contents

Introduction

Way With Worlds was one of those things that I just happened to do. Looking back, it's not surprising I actually wrote it. Twice. Well, three times, if you count putting the second rewrites into this book. Allow me to explain.

Creating worlds has always appealed to me.

I've loved making up worlds since I was young. I can recall drawing and writing at around age eight or nine; *Star Wars* and various science fiction novels inspired me to write fiction. *Dungeons and Dragons* in my teens further fired my creativity, as did a writer's group built around the comic series *Elfquest*. In college I played more D&D, along with *Champions* and other games, and experienced the shared setting of the *Wild Cards* series. I grew up at a time of amazing media that inspired to create my own fiction and games.

Over the decades, I saw how important settings were to stories. The setting, the world, provided background, drove events, and occasionally reigned in bad ideas. Worlds were the real character behind all other stories.

In my later twenties some friends and I created a shared superhero universe, telling stories about it in a self-published newsletter. We made and shared characters and places, interlinked our tales, and built a universe together. That experience put everything else I'd seen in my creative life in context. I saw how a setting came together, how it was maintained, and what it meant.

The setting, again, was the main character. We just focused on characters in the setting as that's how you knew the world. The universe we dreamed up was the foundation.

In my 30's I fell in with a variety of creative people as the internet connected geeks, nerds, fans, and creatives. I did more fiction writing, edited for other hopeful authors, and created **www.SeventhSanctum.com**, a personal website that eventually become a repository of random generators to inspire creative ideas. The internet age further expanded my creative interests.

Around this time **fanfiction.net** came into being, an early multi-fandom repository of fanfiction. To do my part to help writers, I wrote columns on worldbuilding, taking my past knowledge and putting it into something organized – that was the first *Way With Worlds* series.

These columns were my first attempt to codify all the things I learned about worldbuilding, the good and the bad, the things to do and the things to avoid. I won't claim it was the best thing I did, but it seemed that it helped people – and years later I still run into people that say it guided them

The first *Way With Worlds* ended, as all things do. My writing interests changed from fiction to non-fiction. However I kept coaching, advising, editing, and making creative tools for Seventh Sanctum – always looking for a way to help people.

Of course I kept reading and watching and gaming, experiencing fictional worlds in many forms. As I helped others, as I built random generators, I learned more and more about worldbuilding. I was always trying to understand creativity and everything it involved.

Nearly fifteen years later, I got the wild idea to rewrite *Way With Worlds*. Why not, I thought, incorporate everything I'd learned since then? Why not, I thought, re-evaluate my writing and improve it? Why not, I thought, make it better as it <u>was</u> fifteen years old . . .

I also considered making it a book, making it something a bit more permanent. You can probably guess where this is going.

Somewhere around when I started rewriting it and posting it at Seventh Sanctum, I got an email from someone mentioning how they'd printed out my old columns years ago. That struck a nerve with me – someone had printed out my ancient-in-internet-time advice for reference fifteen years ago.

That motivated me to finish the work, expand it, and <u>definitely</u> do a book. If someone felt my advice was worth keeping, I could make it better and more accessible.

When the columns finished, I wrapped them up in a series of books, edited them and expanded them, and made them ready for a broader audience. No longer existing as files on the internet and random musings, the books could even outlast me (a thought that certainly came up as I turned 47 the year the rewrites were done).

You're reading that result.

It's my hope this helps you be a better worldbuilder and creator – be your area stories, comics, games, or something else. The foundation of a good story is a good place for it to happen, so I'm going to show you how to build a *where*.

But enough abut this. You have worlds to build, settings to make, and tales to tell. So let's go, and I'll do what I can to help you get to a place that never existed, and take others there as well.

- Steven Savage
June 15th, 2016

What You'll Get Out Of This Book

So, now that you're diving into this book, flipping through it in a library, or reading a sample copy – what are you going to get <u>out</u> of it?

By the end of this book you'll understand:

- My basic philosophy of worldbuilding – that the world, in a way, is a main character.
- The basic principles of worldbuilding, and the role of worldbuilding in giving a reader or player a proper "feel".
- The way a setting comes together, and especially what it means for intelligent life – your cast.
- The role of Magic and Technology and where they may or may not differ.
- How to create religion and the challenges you'll face.
- The difference between species and races, and understanding how sex and reproduction affects them.
- The role of characters in your world.

In this book you'll find suggestions, advice, and even the occasional exercise to help you out. Put these into practice wherever you can to help you be a better worldbuilder – or find where my advice might not fit you. Everyone's situation is unique after all!

Now that you know where we're going, let's get on that journey to a Better World – in the well-constructed sense, that is.

Why Worldbuild?

The internet age has given us more ways to create and to distribute our creative works. You can build a world for an online game, a role-playing group, or a self-published novel. If you have a world, you can breathe life into it and share it with others through many means.

But there's a question here – why focus on worldbuilding? Why treat it as something unique and separate and identifiable in our creative process?

Well, I have an answer, of course. First, though, let's have a little terminology to help you understand just why this is important.

A Definition Of Worldbuilding

Let's define worldbuilding here for the sake of discussion and possibly argument. I consider worldbuilding to be the following:

1) Creating a stable setting . . .
2) . . . where stories take place . . .
3) . . . that is consistent . . .
4) . . . and works by its own rules.

Worldbuilding creates something *independent* of a story (be that story in a comic, novel, game, etc.). It has its own rules, principles, and so forth. The stories take place *in* this setting, and in turn the story abides by these rules and doesn't violate them.

To be fair, a lot of worldbuilding falls somewhere between "Its Own Rules" and "Whatever I Want At The Time" where continuities may be altered by other factors – anywhere from a marketing decision to a need to update a tale. Worldbuilding is rarely 100% "this world is totally it's own thing," it is limited by aspirations, by time, by marketing decisions, by what will sell (getting paid is an understandable motivation).

What's important is to aspire to create a world that is it's own thing, that's independent. You may not reach 100%, but the closer you get towards that ideal, the more you reap these benefits of worldbuilding.

Let's discuss what those benefits are.

The Benefits Of Worldbuilding

So what does worldbuilding give you? I'm glad you asked, even if I led you here.

An Understandable Setting. A well-designed world that has rules and locations that are stable is one people can understand. Because it makes sense, it feels real – and the stories within that setting are more interesting because of that sense of reality.

Preventing Errors. It is *extremely* easy to start running with an idea in a story or game or comic, and then violate previous elements of your setting. By thinking about (and recording) your world's information, you write a better tale, avoid plot holes, and make a better story. Even if you're not exactly trying to build a consistent world, a little solid worldbuilding makes your life easier.

Find Inspiration. There's something about a world design that seems to inspire a creator; the more you build your world, the more ideas you get. An obscure city mentioned in passing could be be detailed and provide an even richer setting. Answering unanswered questions can move your narrative forward or even surprise you with new story directions. Just looking over the world you've designed may let you free-associate new and inspiring ideas for your creations.

A Bulwark Against Bad Stories. When you know your world, you're less likely to engage in contrivance or doing half-baked stories. Rules you created reign in bad ideas. Parts of the setting you already made can be used or built on – as opposed to just jamming something in to keep the story going.

Avoiding Favoritism. When you take an active hand in worldbuilding, the integrity of the setting becomes a major goal. This is another barrier against bad writing; you'll be less likely to play favorites with a character or contrive particular plotlines because you're motivated to make a good world *first*. If, for some reason, you decide to break your rules (for example, not killing a character because exploring their backstory would be fascinating), the need to rethink continuity ensures such a change is done well and doesn't violate the rules of your world.

(You're creative, anyone would understand wanting to change a few events to get more cool things to write or draw.)

A Different Form Of Writing. Writing fiction, or a game, or so on is one thing. Writing about a setting is quite another. It can be great practice for a different form of writing, one that is more archival and focused on documentation. Worldbuilding and recording the information requires makes you think about what to write down and how to record it. It's essentially "non-fiction writing" about a fictional universe, further building your writing skills and creativity.

An Additional Piece Of Work. I adore books on fictional settings, dictionaries of characters, and maps of imaginary realms. If the world you build becomes famous, release the documentation of your world. It's fun, and it may inspire others. Also if you're looking to make money on your works, I don't think anyone would mind paying for a good book about your world. I've bought a few in my time!

A Contract. Worldbuilding is a kind of social contract between creator and audience. The creator, by working on a strong continuity with rules, imbues their work with meaning because they are saying there is an element a reader/player/viewer can trust. The person enjoying your work can trust the author to make a consistent, involving tale because the setting has that element of being thought through. If you've ever seen people upset with a bad bit of writing, illogical plot twist, and so forth, you know how strongly people feel about this social contract.

So How Much Of This Do I Use?
You've just started a rather large book on worldbuilding. How much of this will you actually <u>use</u>?

Let's turn that question around.

The book is designed to go into detail on what I consider ideal worldbuilding principles. <u>Something to aspire to</u>.

You probably won't use all the lessons or ideas in all your projects. Some won't matter. Some works require shortcuts. Some works are meant to be simple. You may never use everything here – you may not care.

Think of this advice as an ideal. The question is what you <u>aspire</u> to. We've all got different goals.

It's Time To Build
As you can see, there are quite a few benefits to worldbuilding. You can also see why I'm an advocate for the art – and it is indeed its own art. A well-built setting creates enjoyment and inspiration, as does the crafting of one. Also it's fun!

With that out of the way let's move on to some basics of worldbuilding philosophy.

Basic Philosophy

Views, Lenses, And Your True Main Character

Writing your world up is one thing. You can take notes, document everything, draw up timelines, and so forth. That's a matter of technique, imagination, and your ability to write things down obsessively.

Many of us enjoy worldbuilding. I do, as is fairly obvious. There's something marvelous about constructing a setting and seeing it work. There's something wonderful about those records of a place that isn't.

Getting yourself to use all those note and ideas, on the other hand? **That** can be challenging. Sometimes the ideas just don't seem to come to life, but they have to come to life to become a story. The world is easy for some of us; the creation of a work is hard.

Or maybe you have the opposite problem. Perhaps you don't build your world very well for some reason. You find details boring. You don't take the time; you don't think things through. The world may be alive, but it's a shambling half-life without much foundation

Maybe you have neither problem, but you want to really perfect your worldbuilding.

The solution for everyone is to have the right <u>viewpoint</u>.

Good worldbuilding and creating works within it needs the right **perspective**. Just as viewing a character as antagonist or protagonist changes your perspective, you need to adopt the right perspective to make your worldbuilding really <u>live</u>.

That perspective that works for both the enthusiastic and unenthusiastic worldbuilder, both the energized and the unenergized writer? *Your world is actually your main character.*

Setting As Lead

What has worked for me as a worldbuilder, writer, and analyst of creativity over the years is to treat any created setting as the main character. You're really telling the tale of the setting no matter how large or small your cast, or how wide or narrow your perspective.

Every story in your world is, in a way, a tale of that world no matter who the "real" protagonist is. The events that happen affect the world. They come from the past; they manifest in the present; they define the future. The events happening to your cast may be seeded days, weeks, years, centuries, or even further back in your world's timeline. The events that happen after will echo for equally long in your world, even after the main cast is dust.

You as a writer choose what to zoom in on and what tales to tell *in the setting*. You tell a select moment in time, a specific arc of a character. Then, with that perspective, you can bring all your knowledge of the world and the people in it to bear on your tales. The complete power of that wonderful universe you made comes to life in what stories you decide to tell from its near-infinite supply.

Your world comes first because it's **always** there. It just happens to be filled with smaller stories that tell a bit about it, and those are the stories that writers and game creators turn into their books and games. With the world always in mind, you're always returning to the foundation, to enrich it and to understand what you're creating.

Treating your world as the main character also keeps you grounded. It respects your worldbuilding so it's believable (even when fantastical). It respects your writing by making a solid setting for your tales so you're not at the mercy of whim and mindless plot twists. It reminds you constantly of the world you've built, inspiring you as you review the impacts of the tale you're crafting so current stories are believable and future stories make sense.

This bit of anthropomorphism and focus helps short-circuit potential writing flaws such as playing favorites or ignoring a good setting on whim, and lets you leverage your hard work better.

However, it's difficult to enjoy a book or story written from the perspective of "the universe" (not that it wouldn't be fascinating if done right). You're talking about characters people can relate to. So when you focus on world-building, how do you focus on the cast that's relatable?

That's also a matter of perspective. Several of them.

Focus Your Lens

When writing a story in a heavily defined continuity, I think of each character as a viewpoint or a lens that focuses in on certain aspects of your world. A soldier sees enemies even when there are none. An artificial intelligence knows the technology but can't understand people. A detective knows mysteries that are being unraveled in your narrative but not her own heart.

Each character you write is a **view** on the world; rarely do they truly know everything. This only serves to enrich the story and make them more believable in their flaws and strivings (and keeps your reader delightfully guessing).

The main character or characters of your tale (in whatever form) are the viewpoints you write from. They see the world in certain ways, see certain things happen, and relay information to your reader. The challenge is writing from what they see while all the time knowing that they truly don't know everything, yet they may "know" things in a way that truly communicates what's going on to the reader.

I find this approach also enriches writing. Because no character is truly right nor their knowledge complete, you get into the characters deeper, understanding their views. Because no character has to be perfect (nor should they be) you actually get to explore them as characters. It also focuses on writing them as part of a larger world – why are they who they are, why they think like they do, and so forth.

The characters are a manifestation of the setting that the reader or player "rides around in" to experience that setting.

If you are building a world that is used for a multicharacter game or similar media, then you can create an extremely compelling experience. Each "Lens" for each character means the players or player can experience the radically different perspectives in a more interactive way.

The "Lens" approach is liberating and inspiring – and a bit humbling when you realize that **you** are just a perspective on a very big world . . .

. . . Worldbuilding is always a bit about philosophy. Trust me.

Worldbuilding Is About Perspective

Good worldbuilding is about perspective and knowing when to take one and change one. There's your omnipotent author view. There's the characters in your world. There's the main character who may relate the narrative but is really narrating one of many narratives. There's "the world" as it is, filled with people and perspectives.

Being able to take the right perspective when needed frees you when you need to, focuses you when you need to, and lets you deliver a deeper tale in a well-done world. Ironically, that's often through choosing a limited perspective of characters.

Worldbuilding, Principles, And Morals

I love worldbuilding. You can kind of tell by how I wrote a huge series of columns on the subject and then turned that series into books. A lot of what you'll read here how-to, or advice, or exploration, but I'd like to talk the ethical and moral issues about making a fictional setting.

This isn't about making ethics and morals in your world (that comes later). I mean the moral dimensions of good worldbuilding and what you should do as a worldbuilder and author/creator.

This may sound strange; what are the moral issues of creating a fictional setting? Actually, there are plenty.

Managed Commitment

I'm a Project and Program Manager, a professional at organizing things; I'm a certified Project Manager. That certification, the PMP, indicates that I not only had training and took a test, but it is also something I have to maintain and keep up with classes and work. It represents a strong commitment to what I do.

What I do is of an ethical nature. People trust me, due to my titles and career and certification, to do certain things right. The fact I have this certification and title, speaks to my commitment in turn. I'm sure you can relate in your own work.

Being a worldbuilder is a professional commitment. When you take on making a world when you are a writer/creator, that suggests there are certain things you're committed to that you deliver to your audience. To not do this means you will not meet commitments you've made. In short, if you claim to be a worldbuilder and fail, it's an *ethical* lapse as well as a creative one. If you are going to accept the mantle of a worldbuilder and a writer, then you are making promises.

If you have ever been disappointed in a badly-made setting, you know the feeling of betrayal and the sting of wasted time. When you invest time and money in a fictional work, only to discover the world is poorly made, it's a betrayal of your trust.

We can recover from many losses, but lost *time* is perhaps the hardest thing to make up for. If you deliver a world not worth someone's time, you steal something that can never come back.

So, as a worldbuilder, let's look at what you promise you'll deliver.

Worldbuilding Promises There Is Actually A World

Ever read a story where you could tell the author was making up the setting as they went along? You know that horrible, mushy feeling that there's no "there" there? Yeah, I'm sure you have and I'm sure it was awful.

Most of us have come across a story that was just objectionable or plain bad, but had more of a setting than something supposedly "good." This is a reminder that you expect something in the setting to connect to and not just a pile of stuff. Even if the tale told in a well-made world is awful, something is **there** and the creator is delivering on having a setting (if nothing else).

At least that lousy author did fulfill their promise, and we probably go easy on them for their flaws.

When you create a world, you are promising that yes, there is a defined setting there. There's something people can rely on, understand, and experience. There may be mysteries, but even they make sense in the end. You're not wasting their time with something meaningless.

As a worldbuilder, you're promising a *world*.

Worldbuilding Promises The World Has Rules

When you build a world, you're claiming that it has identifiable components; rules that people can understand and make sense of. Magic requires mana; faster-than-light-travel produces intermittent time dilation; and this law firm makes a lot of money due to a contract. This helps make the world comprehensible – the world has something to "hold on to," to grasp the meaning of things and to understand what's going on.

A building is constructed in a given area according to the unique traits of that location. A building has windows, doors, hallways, and so on. It has materials that have certain effects and traits. Your world is established along certain expectations, and has certain rules it operates by that compose the larger setting. A building slapped together without planning is dangerous or hard to navigate; a world without rules leaves the audience lost. You're *building* something, so make sure it's structurally sound and stands strong where you put it.

Rules may not necessarily be communicated directly to the reader/player or however people experience your world. A reader/player who digs deep enough should at least have an idea that something is going on (or at least a good delusion that they got it when they missed the real rules). People can tell if something "works."

A world without rules is really just you yanking things out of the air or select orifices. Nothing can be counted on or relied on – and in turn you're not worldbuilding. You might be good at it, but in the end there's no rules and no world, and nothing to hold on to, and it may fall apart.

Worldbuilding Promises The Rules Will Be Followed

Of course, rules don't mean anything if you don't follow them. When you worldbuild, you promise to follow the rules you've created. It may sound like you're constraining yourself, but it is really more that you are creating something and building upon it. It is constructive, not constraining. An architect can't willy-nilly ignore the laws of the land – or the laws of physics – without creating a nightmare, and neither can you.

That rules will be followed means people can trust you, the author and creator, to follow what you made. They can count on certain things to happen, and thus understand their meaning. Or, when startled at a seeming disconnect, they begin that delicious quest to figure out "why."

Ever have authors suddenly decide a rule didn't matter and suddenly their tale seemed less sensible? Ever watched a video game narrative where the generic Bring Back The Dead magic didn't work in a cutscene? The world suddenly breaks and the trust is gone. What is there to believe in after that disconnect?

When you break your rules you really do break an agreement with the reader/player. When the rules you made go out the window, you basically lied, and you also made your world less easy to understand and harder to rely on.

As a worldbuilder, you promise you'll follow your own rules.

Worldbuilding Promises The World Is Coherent

Worldbuilding is worldbuilding. You are constructing something, like, well, a building as noted earlier. When you make a world, you're committing to make sure the whole thing actually *works* when people read your story or play your game. A good home's doorbell doesn't ring when you flush the toilet; a good story setting functions as expected (even if part of the fun is figuring out what that is).

You promise rules. You promise you will follow the rules. You also promise the world will make sense *if people know what the rules are*. How much they know depends on many factors, but if they figure them out it should make sense.

Like making a building, you promise certain materials, certain structures, certain functions. Together they make a building that will fulfill a given purpose, stay strong, and be navigated successfully. To not have these things means you've created a mess, perhaps a dangerous one. Good ideas, poorly implemented, not reinforcing each other, are wasted.

This is, I think, where worldbuilding too often falls down. You have rules, you follow them, but you haven't constructed them in a way that works together or even contemplated how they relate. If you have, it may not be a sensible pairing or one where things truly work together *right*.

Incoherent worldbuilding is the stuff of many a late-night discussion or in-game argument, and frustration. If your elves are immortal, why hasn't their culture advanced based on retained knowledge? How can this movie star be so famous and yet pass so easily in public? If faster-than-light drive requires this rare element found only in space, how the heck did people get out into space to find it?

You have the pieces; you also promise you'll build the building and make it work right.

How Seriously Do We Take This?

OK, so how seriously do I take this? Especially in areas of creativity and just plain fun button-mashing or sword-swinging entertainment? Let's face it, some of this isn't exactly a case where you need a lot of rules or structure. We're not all trying to be Tolkien or JMS.

I'd say you take it seriously enough to get the job done when people know what the job is.

If you're working on a game that's a general fantasy action game filled with enjoyable tropes, you're not exactly going to be expected to contemplate Dwarven religion in detail. If you do that's admirable, but it's not exactly in the package you're promising of "101 ways to decapitate Orcs."

On the other hand, if you're trying to create a detailed world, you've made a commitment to follow up on your rules and structure in far more detail. You promise a deep experience, and you deliver by building a coherent, explorable, understandable, complex structure of a world. Works like *Babylon 5*, or the *Dragon Age* game series required hard work to deliver their settings.

It comes down to "how much did you promise?" If you go above and beyond, that's great. If you promised a gourmet meal of concept, deliver. When you promise the world equivalent of a nice greasy hamburger, you only have to go so far, but if you do more it's great.

I'm not going to knock the burger, just deliver a delicious one.

How Do We Communicate This?
Finally, there's an issue of communication of worldbuilding the commitments you made. How do you let people know your worldbuilding can be trusted?

Socially we have all sorts of ways to send signals that we're following ethical and moral guidelines. Traditions, rituals, sayings, check-ins, apologizes, and so on are all methods. Such communications are usually unconscious to us, and why we probably get so enraged when we don't see those social signals when we're on line.

For worldbuilding, communicating your intentions is challenging as people will experience your work differently than regular social interaction. You also face the challenge of telling not showing, because outright saying "here's all the worldbuilding I did" kind of ruins the joy of discovery – or seems pretentious.

I can offer some suggestions to help you through this thorny issue, but it does require individual thought.

- Communicate intent. If your story/game/whatever involves intense worldbuilding, communicate you're working on it. Don't brag, but show up front "here's my promise" – perhaps in blog posts or a forward or a nice map on the inside cover. (There's nothing like a map to say "I did at least some work, even if it was paying this artist I knew.")
- Make sure you communicate enough in your story or game that people can figure out the worldbuilding if they put effort into it. It may take careful mapping of plot points, but an intelligent person should get the sense of your rules and structure.
- Discuss your work where and when you can. When people ask questions online or at a gaming session, feel free to communicate enough of the world to assure doubts, answer questions, or intrigue readers or players.
- Build trust. Your works should build trust, so over time people who follow them will learn to trust your worldbuilding – and the above become less of issues. Just don't lose that trust – it's hard to get back.

Worldbuilding is serious business. Indeed, it's a business that involves ethical and moral commitments. Being aware of those will make you be a better worldbuilder and maybe even appreciate the work you do.

Realism

Realism is something that many worldbuilders, writers, and game masters aspire for. That sense of believability is treasured as it makes the media *real* to the audience. Realism is that thing that makes a tale have an edge, a game hit you in the gut, that thing that brings a visceral element to the experience and you're *there*.

I've also heard it called "Verisimilitude." That is perhaps more accurate in some contexts, but also a damned longer and harder word to spell, so I'm sticking with "Realism" in the most general sense. For this section I'll capitalize it to note I am talking about something deeper.

Your goal as a worldbuilder is to involve the audience in whatever media you create, so Realism is something to strive for in your work because that creates involvement. A sense of Realism is also a sign you have been successful in making a good world, and thus a good tale, from it.

However when you ask what this Realism is, you know what we're trying to achieve, it becomes much more difficult. What is "real?"

When you step back from a fiction that seems "realistic," it may suddenly seem rather <u>unrealistic</u>. Yes, you related to that heroine fighting a dragon, felt the fire on your face and smelled the blood. However she was *fighting a dragon*, which isn't exactly a realistic beast. Yet there, in the experience of a good fantasy novel, it seemed real – Realism with a capital "R."

At the same time, just having "realistic" elements in a tale or a game doesn't mean it *seem* real. A world of cars and computers and gritty real-life experiences can seem detached, empty. Real elements in a story don't mean it feels real.

Sometimes dragons are more believable than accountants. Realism is a trickster.

This is because, like any good trickster, Realism has more than one face. It has two, actually. Your world and the tales and games within it need to show both faces to be truly "real" to your audience, no matter how unreal they may be.

The Face Within: Internal Realism

We can read the most outlandish science fiction or magic-drenched fantasy and be lost within it. We can follow things with little connection to our reality and live them. The unreal, the fantastic, the not-yet true can be very real to us when found in a good world and a good tale.

This is because a setting is believable if it has consistent rules and principles that are followed. It may be a realm of clockwork stars and magical cats, but if people can understand this world, they buy into it. We humans like rules, and when we can sense them in a work, then we can believe that work and the setting it is in.

Internal Realism is this kind of Realism – the Realism of a setting that is consistent, if outlandish. It can be understood and analyzed. Because there is "something" there, it can be believed. Because it can be believed, it seems real to people.

But Internal Realism has an equal partner.

The Face Without: External Realism

When wizard cats war among clockwork stars, we may find ourselves cheering the heroine because we understand her motivations. When superheroes romance, their identities conflicting with their love, we relate because we've had our jobs and careers conflict with our love lives. When people who never existed come from cities we've heard of, we "get" them. When we read of the glint of sunlight on a sea that never was, we "see" it.

No matter how untrue or fantastical or made-up, a good world with good characters and a good tale gives us ways to *connect* to the characters and setting. We can relate to characters, feel their pain, gasp in wonder at a description, or nod at a man who never was describing a good Philly cheesesteak.

This is the Realism that we connect to – pain and emotion, location and cuisine, a visual description that is evocative. It is the Realism that connects us to the fictional through experiences we can understand. Everything else may be unrealistic, but there are elements of "real" we connect to.

These places of connection could be real historical events, believable technology, relatable characters, or visceral experiences. They can be many things, but all good External Realisms bridge the gap between us and the fictional.

External Realism in some cases is literally having elements from the real world. In other cases, it may be realistic elements we connect to. Someone may fight dragons, but we relate to her need to keep an armor budget.

Remember what I said earlier about characters as Lenses? Good characters with their own unique perspectives are great for External Realism, because they bridge the gap with the reader or player, no matter how much they're not in the real world.

Realism: The Two Sides Together

Doing both realisms well as a worldbuilder and media creator are worthy goals because they work together. Internal Realism means your world is understandable and External Realism makes your world relatable. Both mean your audience connects to a setting and its characters even if that setting is strange and alien.

If you lack Internal Realism, your world lacks rules, is hard to relate to, and the realistic parts end up floating in a sea of incomprehensibility.

If you lack External Realism, your world is one people can't connect to. The characters aren't relatable, the experiences lack visceral elements, the setting seems lifeless. You could have a wonderful world, but there's no door to get into it.

Together? Together you can have the most fantastical world that people can connect to. They might not consciously realize just how deep they are in a setting that is totally "unreal" because it's so real.

Again, Realism is a trickster.

Getting Both Sides Of Realism

How does one develop both kinds of Realism? I've found these things help:

- **Good World Design.** In short, don't skimp on building your detailed setting. Throw yourself into it and get all those fine details. That is good for Internal Realism.
- **Worlds That Work.** Put your worlds to work and create with them. Push yourself and your creations to see what you can do. Can you write multiple tales in them? Can you write up a description of, say, the magic in a way that explains things understandably? Can you translate characters into the rules of a Role-Playing Game (even poorly)? Play with your world in different forms to get a feel for it and see if you can relate to it in different ways. When you can, it shows there is a real "there" here. Good for Internal Realism.
- **Ask Questions.** Asking questions of why and how helps you flesh out a world, and helps you think like your audience. Good for Internal Realism and External Realism.

- **Empathy For The Characters.** Learn to step into character's shoes so you understand them. Understanding them as you create better characters and write them well, and this means in turn people can "get" them. Good for External Realism.
- **Empathy For The Audience.** Have empathy for your audience. Is what you write readable and relatable? Do your descriptions evoke and inspire? Thinking of how they connect to your work and you world helps you create better -and maybe find some flaws in your work. Good for Internal Realism and External Realism.

A Worthy Quest

Developing both sides of Realism is a worthy quest indeed. It means you'll create worlds and works people truly connect with. These are powerful, affecting, and memorable.

In other words, very real. Or Real if we want to use capitals.

Genres Within Genres

(Compliments to my friend Scott Delahunt, who wrote a column on adaptions that inspired me to do this.)

Genres, as I have heard it said, are reading instructions. We have certain expectations and mental toolkits that, when we read something of a given genre, we use to make sense of them. Whether this is good or bad is perhaps up for debate, the basic truth is there – humans need to understand things, and genres help with that.

I think this is why "genre mashes" like "samurai zombies" and "steampunk romance" are so popular. They engage two sets of expectations and combine them together, giving us both recognizable elements as well as a rush of the unusual, of ideas colliding. It's that sense of things being both recognizable and different, which can bring inspiration, horror, humor, and other intense reactions that we seek.

(Note such mashups may not be truly original – the mashup may be a substitute for originality – but the rush *is* there.)

However, genres are influences in worldbuilding as well. Because we are aware of audience expectations when we build our worlds, tell our stories, and code our games, we adjust what we do to fit what we think the audience will expect. Genre is one of those things that shapes audience expectations – and one that will shape our worldbuilding.

This makes genres a bit insidious as they may limit us and we may not be aware of it. We just start regurgitating tropes, which is not so much worldbuilding as quilting. I'll address tropes elsewhere, so let's focus on how genres affect worldbuilders.

Genres aren't inherently good or bad. They're a way of thinking, a map. I'm going to focus on how genres aren't always what they seem for the sake of worldbuilding – because genres can hide within others.

When you adapt a certain genre consciously or unconsciously, you might be actually adapting a genre *inside* it, or surrounding it. If you're not aware of this you can quickly suffocate your own worldbuilding under the weight of the things you've dragged in unawares.

You're probably going to use genres in our worldbuilding; we can just be more aware. I'd like to focus on a specific issue that affects a lot of genre work: when we pick a genre but actually didn't want that genre, just part of it.

Consider The Western

This concept of genres within genres came when I was contemplating the role of Westerns. As I wrote this originally in 2014 when I thought of westerns, I often thought of what was known as the Space Western.

The Space Western at this time is nearly its own genre. It has its roots in early pulp SF and is obvious in the "Wagon Train" elements of Star Trek: TOS. However, in the last few decades it's become its own thing. Just a few examples came to mind over the decades:

- The movie series *Oblivion*.
- The frontier is referenced strongly in the *Buck Rogers* Role-Playing Game from TSR.
- The television show *Firefly*, the followup movie *Serenity*, and related media.

- The anime *Cowboy Bebop* (which has several other genres grafted on).
- The SF Massive Multiplayer RPG *Wildstar* (which has a gunslinger type class and outright western tropes).

The fact we even have the term "Space Western" to throw around says that it is indeed A Thing.

Now I've got nothing against that. In fact, I've rather enjoyed many Space Westerns, especially self-aware ones. But what I want to discuss is why Science Fiction (SF) is bonded so closely with the Western, as it reveals the dangers of genre-mapping in worldbuilding.

Westerns, at their simplest, are about frontiers. As SF itself is essentially about frontiers in many formats (especially exploration/people on a spaceship stories), the fusion fits perfectly. In a way, Westerns and SF share a similar "inside genre" - that of "people on the edge of the known" - and thus Space Westerns make perfect sense.

However Space Western as a genre – and, as a bit of an overused one, a good example – also shows the danger of overfocusing on genre.

Consider the following scenario:

Maybe your SF story has a frontier element, but Western tropes don't fit it – but if you drag those in unawares (or figure "this just must be a space western") then you're affecting your worldbuilding. Your world is getting buried under tropes and ideas that have nothing to do with your own ideas. You may, in short, figure (perhaps unconsciously) that "my setting is a frontier" and then suddenly you're using the Space Western genre inappropriately, and dumping in elements that really don't fit your setting.

In the end, you got Western when you needed more SF.

This is the lesson. Sometimes you don't want a genre; you want what's inside of it. Or a part of it. Or something similar. You just may get confused over certain genres and *pick the wrong one for your world and tales*.

You need to examine the genres you're working with.

Sometimes It's What's Inside That Counts

Many times we choose or are inspired by various genres and incorporate them into our world, but what we may be looking at is a genre inside the other genre, or a similar genre. If we're not aware of that, however, we'll use the wrong genre or use parts of a "container" genre. For example:

• Maybe you want to do a story of honor and revenge in a world of swords and action. Thus you are inspired by Samurai stories, but the elements of such tales may not fit your world as it has few cultural equivalents. You want honor and revenge, not the cultural complexities of Japanese history.

• Perhaps you want to do a dark mystery in your fantasy setting, and certainly film noir wizards sound cool, but grafting on classic detective elements may not work in a world where you can use necromancy and interrogate the murder suspect (and you may realize this too late into your worldbuilding). You want the mindbending puzzles and betrayal of mysteries, not the film noir elements that would disrupt your setting.

• Perhaps you like the Man Created Monster genre and want to work that into your realistic nanotechnology story when you realize that a giant stompy bad thing is inappropriate when you have micromachines. What you want is to give the threat a *personality*.

Thus when you choose your genre or genres of your world, you may want to ask what you're doing and why. Is it the genre or genres that you want to write – or is there something inside it that you're really aiming for? If you don't realize this, it affects your tale and your world.

Food For Thought

So when you're deciding on your genre(s) ask yourself these questions. What are you . . .

. . . Trying to say? Do/does the genre(s) make sense to what you're writing or are you trying to use what's "inside" one to communicate something.

. . . Really writing? What is at the core of your world? Why are you dressing it up in a given genre? Is it getting buried under the associated tropes?

. . . Trying to communicate to the audience? Genres can provide shorthand to the audience, but is what you're saying actually served by the genre in question?

Genres may be instructions, but they can be limits – and even traps. But sometimes genres hide in genres, so you might not know just what you're doing and why in your worldbuilding. Self-awareness – and genre-awareness – can help you greatly.

World Creation Essentials

44 | Steven Savage

Origins: In The Beginning – Once Again

The next few sections will focus on important, but general parts of your setting that you need to define. This should not be taken as a list of the **only** things you will have to create. Consider them a review of vital basics you'll need to develop when building a setting.

So let's start – with beginnings.

Where It All Begins

Worldbuilding really starts with he origin of the world . . . sort of. We may not always spend time on the beginning of our world when we start building it; we may be following a rush of creativity as inspirations form, but in the end good worldbuilding always comes back to the question "where did it all come from?" Everything has some cause, and just as people have asked "where did I come from" and sought meaning in their lives, your world has to be able to answer that question to have meaning as well.

The answer may not be particularly deep, but the answer is important. It's the foundation of all "whys" that follow.

Your setting may be created by gods, and have a complex pantheon. Your setting may be in our universe and thus be familiar as the daily news. Your setting may be "our world plus something odd," playing on the sense of the familiar and the unfamiliar with new rules. However, your setting has an origin no matter what kind of setting exists.

You want to know how it all started. Why do I harp on this? Well, I'm glad you asked.

Why Know Origins?

Here is why you need to focus on your origins of your setting, in no particular order.

To Know Your Research Materials. Working on your world may mean some research, especially if it's based on science, historical knowledge, classical mythology, and so forth. Knowing your setting's origin, be it Big Bang or Ymir's death, means you know what research is required to define the world. In cases where you're going for "whole cloth" then you at least have an idea of what other references you may need – or what you need to create from whole cloth.

To Know Your Big Issues. When you know the origin of your world, then you know any "big issues" - or lack of the same – and then can ensure they influence your worldbuilding properly. Maybe your setting is the result of a battle of two great alien forces and the fallout and technical ruins affect the story. Perhaps your setting is everyday Chicago with our normal human concerns. Either way, you know what Big Issues strongly affect your world and what do not (though faking out readers or players can be part of the fun).

To Know What To Go Back To. Thinking over your world's origin also gives you something to "go back to" when you lose inspiration, aren't sure of what's going on, or when you need to fill in some blanks in the world. You can do this because you have a good sense of "why" to make sense of your setting and guide you when lost.

To Know What's Important. When you understand how your world came to be, you also have an idea of how much the reader or player needs to know to understand it (even if you plan to keep things mysterious). Knowing the origins tells you what has to be understood to "get" the story or comic or game you made. Just don't spill too much; as noted earlier, characters are good "Lenses" for tales and games, save the big reveals for notes or guidebooks.

To Get A Sense Of "What's Up." Perhaps the most visceral reason to contemplate the origin of your world is that having a sense of "where it all comes from" gives you a general idea of what's going on in your world. Knowing you know "enough" about how your setting, planet, or what have you came into being and what it means provides comfort, inspires you, and lets you have that gut feeling of knowing what's going on. It's hard to explain it – but my guess is you've felt it. I know I have – that sense of "I get it."

So you're ready to go back to the beginning and ask how your world came to be, and flesh it out. Before you fire up your word processor or get out that pencil, the question arises – how far do you go in understanding your setting's origin?

Let's face it, you've only got so much time and you don't want to waste it by doing more than is needed – or waste time rebuilding your world when you didn't do enough.

Origins: How Far To Go?
So how much of the origin of your setting do you need to devise in the first place? Some people can write volumes on their settings (and have). Others, not so much.

It's important to know what you need to define origin-wise because you can overdo it or not develop your world enough. Too much detail means you're really writing a guidebook and aren't actually writing your story or game. Too little and the story falls apart because there's no foundation.

Fortunately, I have some quick rules to help you out.

Right Level Of Detail. The level of detail you want to put in your setting's origins is "as much as you need plus a bit more." Always go the extra mile in putting detail in your worldbuilding origin (in fact, I'd say this is a good rule on worldbuilding *period*). That little extra detail you put in makes sure you don't stop yourself too early and thus avoid enough detail. That little extra also pushes you just a bit farther to keep you thinking, and gives you the comfort to know you designed more "just in case."

Have A Gut Feel. Do you have the "gut feel" that you're comfortable with the level of detail? If you feel confident you solidly know what's going on, then you probably do have enough information. That's where I find the "little bit extra" above helps; it's the icing on the cake, and it helps you say "I got this right and then some." You don't want to keep mistrusting yourself (which so many creative people seem to do).

You Can "Trace Back." "Trace back" is important to origins and beginnings. If you can look at major plots and themes and "trace them back" to the origins of your world, that's a sign you've defined them well. You need enough cause-and-effect to know how the world got to the point in the tales you tell.

There's Inspiration. If you can look at major parts of your origin and easily conceive of other plots and stories, you probably have enough detail. This could be as simple as a glance at the daily news or history in a real-world setting, or asking what happens when your pantheon of gods has an inevitable battle. Think of it as "trace back's" parallel. Can you go forward easily from you origins to new plots? If so, you probably know enough.

Something You Can Communicate. If your origin can be explained to other people, then you know you've done well with it. That means it makes sense, it's communicable (even if communicated from points of views in stories), and you're likely to remember it or understand it if you have to go back to your notes.

Origins are a tricky business, and in my experience they're usually over- or under-done by worldbuilders. This may mean there really is no easy-to-find perfect balance, but that's no reason not to try. The results will create better, consistent, dare I say "well-founded" work.

The End Of Talking Beginnings

Origins give us foundations to our world, and all that comes from that knowledge. They're just a bit of a tricky business because its hard to know how to get the level of detail right. When you take that time, you get all the benefits of a good origin – and so does your audience.

Plus, if you ever publish that extensive guidebook of your game or story world, it's just one more thing to show people . . .

Ecology And Ecologies

So you've got the origin of your universe (or perhaps you used our universe as a template, which does save a lot of effort as you live there). Now that you know how it all began, it's time to design the next level: how the places your characters live in function.

Cosmology is decided. It's time to move to Ecology.

Ecology is a word with a lot of meanings and a lot of applications. For the sake of this book I'm defining Ecology in worldbuilding as how you define how the parts (especially the living ones) of your setting work, relate, and interact. Your stars, soil, plants, animals, biospheres, diseases, and the like. I'll refer to it as Ecology with a capital "E" for referring to the big-picture worldbuilding, and with a small "e" for specifics.

Why Ecology Matters

Ecology is important to good worldbuilding for the following reasons:

Connection: Ecology is the linkage that ties the Cosmology to your characters. It's not just how the universe/world/setting was made, but how it functions and how various phenomena happen like wind, disease, or where edible plants grow. Your characters (the lenses on your story and world) live within this Ecology and are part of it. Knowing this helps you be a better worldbuilder – and create better media.

Foundation: Ecology defines many elements of what happens in your stories because the specific ecologies you write is the living network your characters are in and interacting with and often come from. If a character gets sick or has to fight a monster living in a specific environment, then you're entering questions of Ecology. Thinking about Ecology in your Worldbuilding ensures you've got those questions asked and answered.

Responsive: When you understand your Ecology and ecologies, then your world quite literally takes on a life of its own. Understanding your plants, animals, and biospheres and how they interact means you can properly write the impact of changes on your setting, on the characters within it, and how they may change it. As you build your Ecology, your ability to write it will probably become automatic.

Believability: The first three elements come together to make a world believable. If your characters destroy forests without repercussions, ignore diseases, travel across a swamp next to a desert next to an arctic tundra (unless the world is really a mess) then it's not believable. Thinking about Ecology means the setting you write is one people can "get" because, essentially, it's alive in its own way, and readers can detect the consistency.

(If you're thinking ecologies are like characters, then you're getting it.)

Stimulating: Ecology is something we encounter every day, from the joy of fermented food or an exotic dish to dry skin to fears of disease. Defining your ecology gives you a wealth of knowledge and ideas for stories because your world has those details. A well-defined setting's ecology not only functions on its own, it can take on a life of its own in your imagination and give you great ideas.

Writing And Defining Ecology – Enough
Defining Ecology can be a pretty daunting task, and you'll need to decide how far to go in your worldbuilding. Maybe it's just some general notes or maybe it's extensive research; you'll have to make the call. However, there are also a few rules for writing good Ecologies and elements of ecologies (note the small "e" as we're getting specific):

1) Any ecology, large or small, is about the exchange of energy and matter. The sun and soil feed plants, animals eat plants, animals eat other animals, and so on. A character needs to find water to drink, and a city distant from water needs a source of H_2O to survive.

2) An ecology is about relations. It's hard to separate parts of an ecology from each other. A sure sign you're doing a good job designing one is when you can't figure out when one part ends and another begins. Having predators over-feed on herbivores and destroy their own food source is a grand example of that understanding.

3) Ecologies are dynamic unless your ecology is a "dead planet" (which has a much slower ecology as it is mostly geology). Things may be stable, but it's the dynamic homeostasis of a person balancing on a tightrope – or not balancing, which may be part of your story or comic or game.

4) Ecologies are, to an extent, self-regulating. This could be something as benign as the delicate interplay of animals and grazing plants, or the horrors of a disease that burns itself out as it kills victims too fast. When things get out of whack ecology-wise you have some interesting and terrifying stories.

A fair warning is that you can go pretty crazy with thinking about Ecology (and the specific ecologies) because there's just so many levels of detail that you can get lost in them. At some point you may have to stop yourself unless the insane detail is the point. The basic details for a good ecology are usually:

1) How the various inhabitants you write about survive and function in the ecology/ecologies/Ecology.

2) The major plants, animals, residents, and biomes.

3) How the above relate to each other.

4) What sources of energy keep things going – the sun, magic, or whatever Sometimes an ecology in decline *is* the story.

If you want to get beyond that, it's your call. Just keep the warning in mind that this can get addictive.

A Pattern Emerges
An ecology's tight linkages can be pretty telling. Once you look at the different pictures and connected levels, you start to notice something.

Your characters are in an ecology (a setting), in a larger ecology (a world), and the overall Ecology of the universe is a result of Cosmology. Everything is tied together; you can't disconnect things.

Keep this in mind as you write.

Ecologies: An Example
Let's take a look at how Ecology can affect a story by looking at a small-e fantasy ecology.

Let's say you've got a story with your usual Fantasy rampaging horde of Orcs/Goblins/whatever stand-ins for evil you use. Sure the whole rampaging horde is nice, but what do they eat and how do they survive? These folks are busy rampaging and that burns calories.

If they immolate and pillage everything in their path, then they destroy raw materials, drive away food animals, and have less to survive on. How do they get water for such large armies of slavering monstrosities? Add in the amount of hate they generate (which means people will be trying to stamp them out), and you realize a rampaging horde is a long-term ecologically inefficient thing.

Now if you're a writer (or an Evil Overlord, or both), designing your rampaging horde with ecology in mind makes them more believable. Maybe they survive by being expert hunters (and gain additional skills at stealth and targeting). Perhaps they cache supplies instinctively as a kind of animalistic storing habit. Maybe they only destroy what they can't use, their enhanced senses and strong survival instincts letting them quickly assess what to ruin or take.

Now your rampaging horde is more believable and scary: a species of natural hunters and hoarders who strip towns and encampments bare, wield deadly bows, and move stealthily. It's going to be a believable, terrifying, and fascinating threat.

Your heroes may have to get a lot smarter, ambushing hunting parties, learning their habits, destroying supply caches to stop a retreat. Also, in thinking ecology, you began devising a culture for these rampaging hordes; a smart, savvy one. Maybe your heroes even grow to respect them, and even wonder if they can be turned away from evil . . .

   . . . and any story in your world gets a lot more interesting and believable. Which is the point.

Closing

Ecology and ecologies are a vital part of worldbuilding. Doing them right makes worlds more believable, plots richer, and can help stories almost write themselves. Writing ecologies also teaches you how the parts of a world work together and helps you become a better worldbuilder in general.

Intelligent Life

Let's assume the setting of your story has intelligent life in it. If not, that sounds like a challenging write, and feel free to skip this part until you need it. Or don't because hey, you never know.

If you've got a setting, and stories in it, someone there has enough brains to tell a story about. That's intelligent life.

First, allow me to define intelligent life, so we're on the same sheet of virtual paper here. Intelligent life is a form of life that can process information, use this information, and pass this information on to others. It also possesses a level of self-awareness – this self-knowledge is part of the processed information.

Intelligence must contain a level of self-awareness, as intelligence life is self-modifying and self-directing. You can't separate intelligence from consciousness, because someone has to "be in there" to be intelligent. "I think therefore I am" is also "I know I am as I think."

With that all too brief (and doubtlessly incomplete) journey into the philosophy of intelligence, let's continue as to why it's important in your world. I'll also try not to overdo the words "intelligent life," but no promises.

Intelligent Life: The Focal Point

As noted, you can probably tell a story without intelligent life, but that's going to be a bit challenging. You may also have never considered doing a story without intelligent life. Either way, let's talk about why your worldbuilding will probably include intelligent life – since knowing why will help you design it in your setting.

First of all, writing a story or making a game about sentient life is something most of us do anyway because we *are* intelligent life, despite that incident back in college we hope no one remembers. Most of us are just going create tales about intelligent life anyway as we're used to it and are going to do it anyway. With a good world and proper sentient beings, our stories, games, comics, and so on will be more believable.

You can't take intelligence for granted in worldbuilding or real life.

Secondly, the reason we write intelligent life is that we relate to it; that is a powerful part of good storytelling. An audience needs people to relate to, and it is rather easier to relate to someone you have something in common with – intelligent life. Characters are "lenses" on the world, and it helps to understand that lens.

Third, it's bloody difficult to write a story without intelligent life in it for the first two reasons. Again, you may do it, but not everyone is up for the challenge even if you want to. It's OK! Try it again once you hone your skills at worldbuilding more.

Fourth, your audience may just lose interest if there's no one to relate to or no perspective to relate to. This will depend on your skill as an author, of course, but let us be honest about the limitation.

Fifth, some mediums require intelligent life to "play", such as gaming and certain sims. You can't avoid putting it in your setting in many cases, though again that may depend on how you rise to the occasion.

In short, intelligent life in your world gives people something to relate to, understand, and/or live the world you built.

This raises the question of what kind of intelligent life you're creating. There's three kinds in most settings, and depending on your setting you may be writing all three.

Humans

A lot of settings are going to have humans or the equivalent. If you're writing modern-day fiction you can pretty much just read this section and go on, though you never know as there may be other almost-sentient life in said setting, like computers and golems.

Humans are the defaults for a lot of settings and, in a few cases, the species you create in your world might as well be humans. Humans and might-as-well-be humans are easy to write as we're familiar with them.

If you have humans in your setting, you have the advantage of:

• A relatable viewpoint. Your human "lenses" in your world will be easy to relate to at least for other humans.
• People understand how humans think and work and live as your audience is humans (I assume, at least).
• You can draw on personal experience and other people's experiences to understand your setting and characters since you're human.
• You can draw on human history to understand characters and get ideas. In a few cases, such as historical settings, this may be unavoidable.
• If your world is a real setting, you have a lot of research to draw on created by your fellow humans.
• Sometimes it's just easier as a worldbuilder and a writer to write humans as it's less effort.

The challenges of writing humans are:

- If you're going to have humans in your world, you had better get how people work or you'll do it wrong – obviously wrong. That may seem an unnecessary warning, but think of the moments you or someone else didn't "get" people and imagine that on a world or story scale.
- If your setting is in a real time and place, you'll need to know it **very** well. Otherwise you'll make mistakes – and those will be obvious to your audience.
- You can think you know people and thus not put in the effort to make good characters. Writing humans can make you careless, and can lead to less character building or bad character building.
- If your setting is your own creation, you may stick humans in it without thinking of why they'd be there or how they'd exist in it. In short, you transplant humans into a setting that doesn't quite fit them or fit how you designed them. Your readers/players/etc. will pick up on this.

Maybe your setting goes beyond typical humans or has more than that. That's when you bring in . . .

Human-Likes
We all know the human-likes. They're the species and peoples in novels, games, and settings that are like humans but with some differences. Elves, dwarves, all-too-human aliens, and so on are the Human-Likes that we're used to.

Human-likes are staples of many settings. We're familiar with them from examples like pointy-eared elves and pointy-eared logical aliens.

In making good human-likes, you have to make sure they're human enough to relate to but also different enough to be, well, not too human. Otherwise you're just giving a species funny clothes, a few bits of makeup and calling them "non-humans."

This is going to require you to think about origins, evolution, and biology, quite a bit. The species you're creating may be human-like but they are **not** human and you have to put the effort into designing them.

This is where it starts getting complex, because now you've got to explain why your blue-skinned human-likes are, well, blue-skinned. Or why the species you created has every human emotion except laughter It's a bit of work to have the not-quite-human species in your setting, and you may not notice this as you figure "hey, close enough."

In making human-likes you have to ask about:

- Their evolutionary/created origins and backgrounds – why they are like they are (and why they're like us).
- Where do these species differ from humans, why, and what is the effect of these differences on them?
- How do they interact with their environment and others in ways that are and are not like the humans we know?

Work aside, human-likes are useful for many reasons in our settings, these being the specific advantages:

- They're still as relatable or almost as relatable as humans. They make good lenses while having lots of interesting variance.
- Their differences from humans can be interesting to explore in your worldbuilding and writing. Exploring immortality or long-life, unusual abilities, and so on that deviate from the human experience can be fascinating.

- You can still draw on personal experience, historical research, and the like to create and write them; you just need to be aware of the differences.
- If you're writing legendary or mythical characters, you have those sources to draw on, though I recommend doing your research to ensure you don't embarrass yourself by making assumptions. Those legends can be tricky and aren't always like we assume they are.

The disadvantages of creating human-likes into your world are:

- You can end up making them too human and you might as well have written people. This also breaks believability in your setting as it looks contrived.
- You can make them seem human enough but take such a left turn into "elsewhere" that you give readers whiplash. Grafting on radical differences, as opposed to understanding how they work in your setting, can cause this. Know why something is different from humans and what it effects are.
- You can make them too generic and end up with the infamous "guy with some makeup on his face" aliens or a planet where people just wear a different hat. Unless there's a reason for everyone to be too alike, make sure your human-likes are as unique and interesting as real people are.
- As noted, you may not put enough effort into making them their own unique people and not just humans-with-something-else.

You may, of course, want to play some serious setting hardball and not create humans or human-likes, or create more than them. That's when you get to . . .

The Unique Intelligent Species

Now you're talking. Your setting is going to have one or more unique intelligent species that aren't like us at all. This is when you pull out all the stops and have a lot of worldbuilding work to do.

If you're going to put unique intelligent life in your setting, consider the following questions to help you out:

- What was the role of the species in their ecosystem before they were sentient (if they were ever non-sentient)? What is their role and impact now?
- How did the intelligent species evolve, if they did evolve? What traits are retained from their evolutionary past physically, intellectually, and emotionally?
- How did the species become intelligent? Evolution? Creation?
- How does the species survive in its environment or environments, and what role does intelligence play?
- If the species was created, by whom (and what is their background)? For what purpose, and how do they fit that purpose, and how is that reflected in their life? They're not machines (metaphorically); they are sentient, but someone made them for a reason and that will affect them.
- What role does their intelligence play in their lives overall, from what they enjoy to how they interact? This adds many juicy possibilities: they could be created; the intelligence may be a side effect of magic or mutation; or they may have had to adapt quickly to environmental changes.

A unique intelligent species takes a *lot* of work to design. This is where doing your research on science, biology, myth, or whatever foundations of your world exist in order to understand them. This is where you've got a lot of thinking to do. It's also why I emphasized so much work on understand the origin and ecologies of your world, since here's where you'll really use it.

One side effect of this is that when you do it, you really think about your setting. When you're up for creating a new species in your world, you're going to get truly intimate with the universe you've created. That's a nice extra benefit for all that work.

More reasons to design unique intelligent species in your world:

- It makes sure the species truly fits your setting.
- It's more interesting as everyone isn't a human wearing a funny bit of makeup.
- It makes a setting richer, and thus believable.
- It avoids the issue of shoehorning in humans and human-likes into an inappropriate setting.

The risks you face in making truly not-human species:

- It takes work and thought. Messing this up or doing it half-way makes an inconsistent world.
- It takes skill to do right. You may need to build up for it.
- You can make a detailed, understandable species that no one can relate to in your tales or game or whatever and that you can't write. Design can lead you to something with no Lenses.

Closing

Creating intelligent life is a challenge, even when you're just pretty much copying and pasting humans. However it's a vital part of your setting because the intelligent characters are the ones people experience the story through. It may take research and developing skills to truly push your abilities to make believable intelligent species, but the rewards are a relatable and intriguing world.

Culture And Civilization

Thanks to heavy worldbuilding you've got your setting, and in that setting you've got intelligent life (probably). Now that you've got sentient species in your universe, it's time to work on their Culture and Civilization. I'm capitalizing deliberately, by the way, just like I did with Ecology, to remind you this is an abstract discussion.

Culture and Civilization are something everyone takes for granted because people are used to *living* in them and with them all the time. Intelligent life and culture are inseparable, and thus a big part of the worlds you will make.

Let's start with looking into just what Culture and Civilization actually **are**.

Culture And Civilization – What's Being Talked About Here?

What are Culture and Civilization? I'll go and give some quick summaries, but of course we're talking about concepts people have debated for ages. So these are viewpoints towards applying these concepts to worldbuilding, not to answering age-old questions. But I figure I'm right anyway.

Culture – Culture is those things sentient life learns and passes on among its members so they function, work, relate, interpret, and so on together. Culture is not just shared knowledge, it's knowledge that helps people define themselves in relations to other people and other things.

Civilization – Civilization is when you really kick things into high gear Culture-wise. You start building things, establishing centers, and writing your culture deep into your physical environment. I'd say that you need a culture to have a civilization, but then again there's some pretty interesting worldbuilding to be had by violating that rule.

Metaphor-wise, I think of Culture as the operating system and programs that run in a sentient being's mind. When we start seriously connecting cultured people together and modifying the environment, establishing things that last over time, then you've got a giant interlinked system like a manufacturing system or computer network – *that's* Civilization.

You can also see why culture and civilization is vitally important for good worldbuilding:

- They are things that you would expect intelligent life to have. Admittedly, as of this writing the only intelligent life we humans have to compare any worldbuilding to is us, but still – you go with what you know.
- Culture obviously affects how your characters see the world and how they'll interact with it. It gives perspective, so knowing it gives you and those experiencing your media perspective.
- Because Culture is how intelligent life gets perspective, it is part of how each character is a Lens on your world. Knowing your setting's culture or cultures is not just good worldbuilding, it's indispensable for storytelling. If a culture is hard to comprehend that may require some delicate writing, and may produce an epic tale of a truly unique world that sucks people in.
- Culture and Civilization are huge parts of the stories you'll tell in your world, and in some ways *are* the stories. They are the reasons people do what they do, the reason things happen, A simple look over any story, comic, or game will show how much motivation and happenings are because of the structure of a culture and/or the civilization it built.

- People expect them. Because they are something an audience is so used to, their very lack will sit ill with them – unless that lack is, again, part of the setting, and you engage in drawing people into that setting.

So with this said, let's get to building.

Crafting Culture

Creating the culture or cultures in your worlds is probably something you're doing automatically, often for the aforementioned reasons. But I find it helps to have an idea of what we're doing to keep us inspired, focused, and not losing track of what we're doing.

Culture is that which intelligent life creates, relates with, and passes on. You can also think of it as a kind of "improved genetics" where intelligent life has the power to change and grow itself, and pass those changes on. These changes alter and improve not by generations, but by interactions between individuals and the environment.

I'd even go so far to say truly intelligent life has to have Culture for it to do much. Having seen how we humans create culture almost instinctively, I think our limited sample set here makes an impressive example.

So this gives us a starting point for designing Culture: it's how people (be they human or not) work together in the present and the future and communicate and store information. A bit of a cold metaphor, but effective, and it provides good guidance for the worldbuilder.

When building a culture, you'll want to focus on:

- What are the values of the traditions, languages, and peoples, and why do they exist? Why did they develop, or why were they consciously developed?

- How is culture passed on and why is it passed on? How are its elements seen as valuable?
- How does the culture deal with disruptions or with parts of it wearing out? Does it have the ability to adapt?
- What keeps the culture functioning? If it doesn't have its own safeguards, it could malfunction, which of course would be an interesting tale. Cultures do break down in the real world, after all.
- Beings will have a culture that leverages their traits as a species. How does that fantastic sense of smell or natural telepathy affect a culture?
- How is it "prosthetic" - how does it make up for any limits the sentient beings who are part of the culture have? We humans use technology to live anywhere on the planet and that's part of our culture.

You can also drill down into the specifics of culture, like religion, language, and so forth. We'll see about doing that later, but for now this should get you thinking.

Next, let's think of what happens when you extend culture into something more permanent – Civilization.

Civilization – Going Big

Civilization is when Culture settles down and really gets going. In a lot of cases, this is literal. Civilization is when people put down roots, build things, and make a more solidified place to "be." It's what happens when Culture gets physical in the forms of cities, temples, written language, and more.

The software sort of makes its own hardware – sort of like how we humans will make computers with design software to design new computers.

It's hard to extract Civilization from Culture, but in general Civilization seems to be associated with intense physical infrastructure. So for the purposes of this book, I'll consider Civilization to be what happens when Culture becomes more established both physically and intellectually.

Not all your intelligent life in your setting will have Civilization. Culture exists before Civilization, and one doesn't need organization, centralization, or much of a physical infrastructure to have Culture. The first question you have to ask about any intelligent life you design is how far are they into Civilization from just having Culture. A population of nomads or wanderers may have Culture but not what we'd recognize as Civilization.

When Culture gets solid, then you have Civilization.

Civilization in your settings brings in so many other issues that, like culture, one could write hundreds of thousands of words on the subject. But as a handy guide to save you from that, here's a quick checklist for designing your civilization.

- Civilization is culture solidified. You'll want to know at what point (if any) a culture started putting down the roots, policies, buildings, and so forth that turned it into a civilization.
- Civilizations are about stability. They may fail at it, but Civilizations with their complexity and infrastructure represent a chance of more stability than a culture.
- Civilization changes the environment. Farms require irrigation, buildings require quarried stone, industries pollute the air, and so forth. Civilization has impacts not often expected – which can mess with that whole "stability" thing.
- Civilization extends Culture. A Civilization can wield more cultural influence on others, and indeed is usually larger than any independent Culture.

- Civilizations are much more complex than Culture. It's safe to say few people in a Civilization know how the whole thing works. You're going to need a gods' eye view as well as understanding individual perspectives. You also need to make sure a civilization is believably complex in your worldbuilding.
- Civilizations are linked to technology; they require technology to be established, and of course help evolve it.

Big Job, Big Perspective

When it comes to designing Culture and Civilization, you've got quite a job cut out for you. So beyond all the other advice, here's what I recommend.

Study real cultures and real civilizations.

Really, that's it.

Studying other cultures than your own, about civilizations that have come and gone or on their way up or out, gives you an intuitive grasp of how people and their social structures work. At some point you'll probably get a good enough grasp to build your world or get out of a case of worldbuilder's block. But read, watch, listen, whatever.

Besides, it'll broaden you as a writer and a person.

Closing

Culture and Civilizations are inevitable in your world when you're building your setting's intelligent life. They're part of being an intelligent species, and you not only can't avoid them in most cases, you really don't want to as they drive the plot.

It's challenging, but with work and good study, you'll be up for it. My guess is if you're doing any worldbuilding you already started it – just work on doing it consciously.

Economics And Economies

We've talked origins, ecologies, and sentient life in your settings. We've discussed the culture that your intelligent life will doubtlessly have. Now it's time to get to economics which, much like real life, has a lot of impact but isn't something we often think of (or think of fondly).

My guess is that upon hearing that "it's time to discuss economics", you're probably not filled with enthusiasm. If you are, **great**, but economics is not compelling to many people. Perhaps it's boring, frustrating, or recalls classes we really didn't do well in. So I'll assume we should go forward with the assumption that you're not interested in economics, and I should make sure it's engaging and less boring.

If you do enjoy economics (like me), then read on anyway just in case, and welcome to the club of econogeeks. We're rarities; we have to stick together.

Even if you don't get into the economics of worldbuilding, with the right perspective it can be not only useful, but interesting, fun, and informative. I also would note that it can't be completely avoided because, like real life, economics is everywhere. But I'll focus on keeping it interesting just for your sake.

(I'm also not capitalizing economics here as the term is abstract enough.)

What Is Economics?

Economics can be described in many ways, but for a worldbuilder my summary is that economics is where culture/civilization, intelligent life, and the ecology intersect.

- Life needs to extract goods, energy, and resources from the environment to survive.
- Intelligent life may engage in more elaborate resource gathering such as mining, hydrogen farming, dragon egg collection, whatever.
- Your intelligent life needs to exchange goods and services among each other as it is doubtful any single being is independent. There is trade.
- Because they're interacting with each other, that becomes part of culture as it's important to preserve the best way to do these interactions. Institutions, policies, and ethics evolve to do so. This is your basic "economics," however . . .
- Your environment thus shapes the culture of the intelligent life because of what is and isn't available. The world and how one survives in it are always part of culture (or should be, though a culture unable to interact functionally with the ecology is a great and perhaps familiar tale).
- Your intelligent life is shaped by the ecology, and their interactions with each other are shaped by the ecology they live **in**. In turn what they extract from their environment may alter it. There is a feedback loop.

As soon as two members of whatever intelligent species you create trade sharp rocks and furs you get an economy. As you've been building your world, you've probably been creating a lot of an economy anyway – you just didn't think about it.

(That ignorance may have even helped if you find economics boring.)

Looking at economics in worldbuilding as the life/culture/ecology intersection helps you write better simply because it makes you ask what's going on and how things work. It's removed from dismal ivory tower economic theory, boring statistics, and the hyperactive economic pundits. It becomes about the world, which is what you're building anyway.

With this perspective – that economics is the intersection of life and culture and ecology – it's time to create economics in your setting.

Building Your Economies

When you're building the economic part of your world, taking these three elements – intelligent life, culture, and ecology – is what you need to create your economies.

There's a good chance you've already build something of an economy into your world anyway. It happens almost automatically, even if it's just grafting on a lot of assumptions to your setting. In time, good worldbuilders will develop the skills and abilities they need to build the economic parts of their settings and it becomes automatic. I'm writing this with the assumption you need some help, or may not know how much you know.

A great way to build any setting and story is to ask and answer questions. So here's the questions you'll want to answer when building your economy:

Sentient Life:

- What does the sentient life need to sustain itself (assuming, of course, that it has a survival urge)? How is that extracted from the ecology? What are the repercussions of this extraction?
- How aware is your sentient life of the impact it has on the ecology and the impact the ecology has on it? How has this been integrated into their culture?
- Has the sentient life developed any disciplines or theories on economics based on their experiences? How are these influenced, and how do they help or hinder them?

Ecology:
- Can the ecology sustain what intelligent life is doing to/for/with it?
- What limits does the ecology place on intelligent life, and is the intelligent life aware of it?
- How is ecology changing as the intelligent species interact with, exploit, and sustain it?

Culture:
- How much of the culture is influenced by economic concerns and concepts, and how rational are they?
- How does the culture support intelligent life's ability to keep getting what it needs from the ecology? How does it hinder it?
- Does the culture involve any long-term planning to deal with ecological and cultural changes that may shock the economy?
- Is there a good sense of history in the culture of past economic good and bad times, and how do the characters react to that knowledge?

When you're developing the economic parts of your world, you may also find yourself confronting a lot of real-life questions and your own assumptions. That's good, because one reason that economics is so dismal in our world is because it's more a near-religious faith than actual policy and understanding. When your worldbuilding surprises and shocks you, you're doing a great job – more so when it involve the oft-dismal science of economics.

You may even learn a few things. One wishes a few supposed "economists" wrote more fiction deliberately as opposed to the accidental fictions they too often churn out.

But while worldbuilding, you might want to get into levels of details, get more information, and expand your horizon. Maybe you even get into this, or maybe you need help thinking this over . . .

Getting Into Details

If your *really* want to do some hardcore economic worldbuilding, you're better off finding out about real economics. In our world. Fortunately there's plenty of ways to do that that don't involve sitting in a class and falling asleep, or wondering if some economic expert is necessarily insane (hint – if he's yelling all the time and uses sound effects, then yes, this person is bonkers).

A few tips and resources if you want to dig in deep:

History. Books on historical periods relevant to your writing or similar to your writing are usually pretty informative. Economics always rears its head, whether it's logistics for an army or how you build a new temple. You'll also have a lot of fun learning about economics this way since it's tied to culture, ecology, and history.

Documentaries. Grab some DVDs, hit the library, or go on a streaming video service and look for relevant documentaries on economics. You can even play these in the background while doing your worldbuilding to see if anything is absorbed by osmosis. I recommend history documentaries, oddball documentaries relevant to your specific interests, and shows about people's careers. That's where you learn how real life works.

Real Economics. If you're up for it, actual economic texts, videos, and blogs may give you the information you need. It may take some research to find someone reliable, but it's usually worth it. You probably don't need to go this far unless it's a serious part of worldbuilding or if you've gotten bitten by the research bug.

Trace Back. This is a great way to do some serious economic worldbuilding. Pick a subject you want to learn on and dive into it deeply. Want to understand colonization, or when/why gold was valuable, and so on? Pick a subject and figure out "why." This is for dedicated worldbuilders, but it can be educational.

A fair warning, research usually challenges your own economic assumptions. As a worldbuilder, of course, that's awesome. After a while it may even get addicting. Speaking of . . .

So When Do I Stop Designing My Economy?

Some people may have trouble getting to work on the economics in their world, but after a while it can be hard to stop. More and more ideas seem relevant, more and more details get thrilling. Just as someone can over-describe a magic system or faster-than-light technology, people can eventually get into amazing detail about economics in the setting they've created.

So when do you stop building your economy so you can get on to other stuff. Or to write your story or make your game?

First, apply my rule of "what you need plus a bit more." Stop yourself when you've done enough economic design plus a bit extra as a "buffer." I'd say you've gone far enough when you're comfortable that you know how your world works, and then a bit more in detail just to be safe. Even if it's painfully boring to get that extra, do it. You'll probably be happy you did.

Second, another sign you've got a good enough grasp on your fictional economy is you have enough to have a reader understand what's going on if you explained it, but you've also got those little extra details that give the economy life. Economics is alive – trade wars, goods being shipped, and more. If your world has that life, it's a good sign you've got a good grasp of the economy.

Like a good character, an economy feels *alive*.

This is a challenging call, like much any other aspect of worldbuilding, but I usually find the gut feel you get of "OK, that's enough I truly 'get' this" is a good measure.

Now again you may been having fun. Go for it! Just remember the difference between worldbuilding and story telling.

Closing

Worldbuilding economics is usually best done by asking what economics really is (to remove us from assumptions and the threat of boredom), asking questions about the factors that bring our economics together, building our worldbuilding abilities, and learning what we need to know. You'll kind of notice I'm a bit down on "general" economics here.

That's simply because the problem that often plagues humanity will also plague your writing. Too much of economics is B.S.

So go and dig into your worlds economics and ask what's really going on, what's really happening, and why. Challenge your assumptions, create your world. It'll be more believable than many worlds, and probably many in-theory economists.

You'll likely learn a lot as well.

Pyramids Of Power

Have you ever read a story and things just seemed to work . . . wrong in the world?

- The hero/ine defeats one guy and then the world is safe, the Evil Army is destroyed, he gets the girl (or the guy), and his (or her) chin is still awesome? Seems an awful lot happened due to a few actions.
- The superpowered alien who somehow manages to release massive, colorful, well-animated attacks that just well . . . have no side effects, no source, and no real explanation? For example, how do you release a "gravity buster" without messing up everything but the guy you aimed it at? You just busted *gravity* (whatever *that* means).
- The villain who's massive, complex plot works perfectly, while in the real world you aren't even sure the game you're working on will ship without a day one patch and an apology? How does he get *that* to work?

You know that feeling. Things happen easily in stories and games – **too** easily. Cause and effect apparently are having a trial separation and you worry they're going to get a divorce before the book ends. Simple actions have massive and unwarranted repercussions, while large actions have none. We snicker, we laugh, we roll our eyes – and we're out of the world because things just work *wrong*.

Things are more or less powerful than they should be. The influences are wrong.

A lot of worldbuilding is about Power, in the non-stereotype-Machiavellian sense. Power is about how an action produces a result, and when you don't make it work right in your world, then your world is no longer "real." If action and result don't come together, the world doesn't work right.

Power done wrong, from super attacks to a clever cutting comment, makes a world unbelievable. If you're building and writing in a setting, you want to make sure the world seems believable. In building your world, you have to get the power of things, of people and weapons and comments and plans, right or the world is back to being words on paper or pixels in a game.

Fortunately, I have a rule for getting it right. I call it the Pyramid Of Power. Which is a useful rule, and not the place Kephr-Ra, The Never-Dying, hid the Staff of Omens.

But it does sound awesome for a villain base. Just saying.

Power, Process, And Pyramids

The first rule about writing about Power: *Nothing happens without a reason.*

Now that seems obvious in worldbuilding. The problem is making sure that things happen for the *right* reasons, and in turn that actions have believable and appropriate effects. When you lack this appropriateness your world is suddenly not "real" for the duration, but a flawed artistic construct that makes your reader or player go "huh?"

"Huh?" takes people out of the world, and that means you failed as a worldbuilder and creator.

Something should have an effect appropriate to its power – be that the power of an army, the power of a well-timed single word, or an assassin's bullet. Each of these things has an effect that, properly created in your world and portrayed in the relevant media, is appropriate, believable, and understandable.

In general, the more powerful something is, the better you need to understand it, explain it (if only to yourself), and to write it into your tale. The punch of a standard human doesn't need to be explained; the coolness of ice is understandable. The psychic blast of a mutant requires some thought and explanation, as does a weapon that drops temperatures to zero Kelvin while running on house current.

The more effect something has, the more you need to think of it and explain it in your worldbuilding. Again, this may be only for yourself, but as I've stressed, you need to know how your world runs, even if readers or players don't see all the turning gears. It's when the gaps in your concepts show you have problems, when you accidentally give people a peek behind the curtain – and there's something shoddy there.

When you don't think power through, the chance of people seeing the shoddiness increases. Here's a few tips to help.

First, I view Power as a pyramid. The higher it goes (the more powerful), the more of a foundation you need – and the more it affects the foundation of your setting:

- If your hero wields a god-like extradimensional force, then you have to ask the repercussions of that force existing (like other people using it).
- A massive evil secret conspiracy is going to require an awful lot of resources and communications and, well, secrecy. How *does* Anaconda Admiral feed all of his troops in the secret organization of S.N.A.K.E. anyway?

The explanations may be general, and you may only have to go so far, but they will affect and define your world, because some of these pyramids get pretty big.

The higher the pyramid, the bigger the base, and the more you need to explain – at least to yourself. However enough, should be revealed to your audience so they believe it.

Secondly, you have to ask how the pyramid holds together – the bigger it is, the more you have to know how it keeps its form. How does a giant army actually stay ordered, not have mutinies, and remain a credible threat? What safeguards are on the doomsday device? Yes, that alien species is benevolent, but why is their visit not causing massive civil unrest?

How does Power exist, in short, without the Pyramid crushing everything else and falling apart?

All of this requires explanation, exploration, and worldbuilding.

To be brutally blunt, you can probably get away with less worldbuilding around familiar concepts like superheroes, psychics, and serpent-themed conspiracies led by a guy with obvious rage issues. People accept certain tropes easily. However, if you do this too much then your world will only be tropes and you risk it not coming to life or becoming stereotypical. It will be accepted but not necessarily *alive*.

Looking at how Power works, on the other hand, brings your world further to life, and makes it living, believable, and involving.

I find you can also understand Power better when you realize there's two forms.

Two Forms Of Power

A convenient way to look at power is to think of there being two basic kinds: force and subtlety. These are two "pyramids" you may build in your worlds. Yes, it's generalized, but that's the point of rules-of-thumb.

Power Of Force

Force is easy to write, almost temptingly so. The army crushes a kingdom, the hero kicks the bad guy's backside six ways to Sunday, or a mass media campaign sways an election. Big onslaughts and powerful face-punches work, and are also pretty believable.

The Power of Force is of use massive power to achieve results; sometimes the power is even more massive than the result achieved. Think of it as when the Pyramid of Power is dropped on top of something.

When writing the Pyramid of Force, there's two important questions to ask:

How is the force that is used powered/achieved? Massive force requires massive resources of some kind. Something feeds the army, something powers the Planet Cannon, and someone provided the money for the campaign. When you work with sheer force you have to explain where it comes from; because the power is massive, it has to be believable to those participating in your world. A poorly created Pyramid of Force really stands out because the sheer result doesn't line up with how it's part of the world.

What are the side effects? Brute Power is not subtle, and there is almost always side effects and repercussions. Force brought to bear means reactions occur. Force changes the world, and massive overwhelming force produces a lot of changes.

But maybe you're not writing massive armies, fleets of planet-destroying starships, or tales of massive monied efforts. Maybe you're more subtle . . .

Power Of Subtlety

Subtlety can be forgotten in worldbuilding, since now and then a good punch-up or military campaign is more interesting. But the subtle achievement of goals, the knife-in-the-dark, the clever deduction are powerful indeed. Some genres are all about the Pyramid of Subtlety, such as detective stories and comedies of manners.

Subtlety is the force of precision, of asymmetric Power. It is not overwhelming, it is not a bombardment from orbit or a plasma beam in the face. It is a great achievement where the specific action seems small compared to the result, but the result is equally massive. It's the kind word and the strike to the sensitive nerve.

Of course, writing the origin and use of subtle Power is a bit different than overwhelming power. Subtle Power is often diffuse and mysterious, yet also has the element of focus to achieve just the right result. Creating the Pyramid of Subtlety is when you have this big pyramid and stick someone with the pointy part – but you have a big foundation to *get* the pointy part.

When writing Subtle Power, here are three rules to help you:

Subtle Power is usually about bringing all the right elements to bear in a manner that gets an exact result. It is the revolution caused by assassinating the king or the charming word that lures someone into the bedroom. In many ways, the power that makes it possible is far greater than the action taken. The novelist who starts a revolution studies great writers for decades and distills centuries of knowledge, or huge amounts of money creates a tiny virus that kills only the Evil Alien Commander so his people are free.

Subtlety is usually about someone working a critical point. The the right clue, the exposed enemy in the sniper's scope, the clever deduction that solves a mystery. It is about vulnerability and opportunity in the world.

Subtlety's foundation is less obvious. Subtle Power often has a big foundation (like Force does) but it's not as obvious. The assassin who ends a war has twenty years of experience. The clever speech calls upon widespread cultural archetypes to change people's minds. Subtle Power's foundation is large, but not *obvious*.

Subtle power is a strange beast to communicate. The Pyramid of Force's sheer lack of subtlety also invites broad explanations - "we feed the army this way." Subtlety's very nature makes it harder to understand when creating and when experiencing in media, so it takes deft planning.

I find that for many a reader, well-built subtle Power is also very satisfying. It has a puzzle-like quality that speaks to our need to figure things out. So when you define subtle power in your world, you'll not only build a good setting, but your readers and players can enjoy that subtle rush when they see it all come together.

Closing

Creating and understanding Power is vital to good worldbuilding because explaining how things are achieved and done, what repercussions things have, is important to making the world believable. If you don' do this your setting is at best just tropes, and at worst one people can't relate to.

Thinking over Power, and remembering the greater the Power the greater the explanation and repercussions, helps you understand things better and build a better world.

In time I find this becomes an instinctive part of worldbuilding. Soon you're able to see the flows of power and results – and your worlds create themselves and tales can write themselves more easily. It takes practice, but it's well worth it.

Magic And Technology

A Look At Magic And Technology

We've all heard the saying that goes "Any sufficiently advanced technology is indistinguishable from magic," made by the incomparable Sir Arthur C. Clarke. The saying is the third of "Clarke's Three Laws" of prediction, and is the most well known probably because of the whole "magic" part.

I would add an additional law, especially in the worlds of worldbuilding (and perhaps in an age of mind hacking and psychological techniques, our own). "Any sufficiently organized magic is indistinguishable from technology."

This isn't just me being sarcastic, though there is always the chance.

When you worldbuild, you're getting things organized in your head to explain how that world works. In the case of Magic and Technology, when it comes to fiction, they're usually the same thing from a worldbuilding standpoint. Not always, but almost always.

For the sake of *building a setting*, magic and technology are no different. Magic and technology are the ways characters manipulate themselves and the elements of their settings to achieve results fitting a specific goal and thus are really no different. We may use different terms for them, and they may have different relevance to the real world, but magic and technology are just Making Stuff Happen.

One may use ethereal forces and the other uses vacuum tubes, but both are about results and are largely the same for the sake of worldbuilding. To avoid speaking about them by calling them "Magic and Technology" over and over, I'll call them "MaT"

As a worldbuilder, you just have to figure out what MaT is, how it works, what it means.

Magic, Technology, And Setting

So where does MaT fit into everything in worldbuilding? Actually that's the thing – it fits into *everything*.

Intelligent Life: If you have intelligent life, you usually have MaT. Intelligent life almost inevitably alters itself and its environment while trying to survive and prosper inside of it. Intelligent life is the source of MaT or at least its use – someone may not invent a piece of MaT, but they may use one.

Ecology: MaT affects and is affected by the ecology of the world, be that an ecology of hard science or supernatural forces. MaT is what you get when intelligent life takes whatever makes the universe go and decides how to make it go in a given direction; because much or all of that power comes from the ecology, it brings in many limits and other factors. Pollution may be a problem, draining the magical forces out of an area another, but it's all ecology.

Origins: MaT builds on the foundations of the origins of your setting, from hard science to timeless gods whose power can be called on. MaT is not outside the setting (or the larger setting), it exists by manipulating the setting.

Culture: Culture lets MaT be passed on, enhanced, remembered, – or corrupted, forgotten, and misused. MaT also affects culture because it can be used to establish cultural elements, build places, transmit information, and so on. In many ways culture is inseparable from MaT.

Economy: Cultivating plants, building roads, or transforming gold by calling upon sea spirits all relate to the economy of your setting. MaT is inseparable from the economy as well because MaT affects, and is affected by, the economy it exists in whether it influences or just plain destroys.

MaT is pretty much part of anything you're creating setting-wise. In your own worldbuilding endeavors you've probably been designing a lot of spells, starships, or super computers anyway. This is just a good reminder that it may go even farther than you realize.

Questions To Ask

So with that being said, how do you design it? It gets pretty overwhelming when you look at all you have to build, even though most worldbuilders probably dive on in. What I do is recommend asking questions to get your mind moving or to move it in the right directions.

Question #1: Why Was It Made?

MaT solves a problem, or is at least assumed to do so. So, in your setting, ask: why a given spell, gizmo, or discipline was ever made in the first place? What problem does it solve for your characters, civilizations, or cultures?

In plenty of cases, the reasons something exists are obvious, from a spear for hunting to a psychic discipline to stop predatory entities. In other cases some things may not be so easily explained or sensible, so thinking about why something was made helps thoroughly understand it, or understand why it's not a fit for your world.

Remember, when asking this question what your cast and culture things are the reason something exists isn't always the reason others may think it exists. Things are re-purposed, MaT fails at one solution but is applied to another, or simply some inventor is just scamming people.

There's why, what it's used for, and what it was originally designed for.

Question#2: Who Made It, Makes It, And How Is It Made?

Who makes the computers, builds the starships, creates the spells, and so forth? Where does it come from?

This is extremely important as MaT has to be produced or made in some fashion so people can use it (even if they stopped making it). Does it take craftsmanship, or can you go to a store? Are spells wrung from ancient grimoires or do you download a file off the internet? Are starships made by automated factories, or is technology lost and everything is re-purposed?

Asking how something comes to be tells you a lot about how hard it is to get, how it is regarded, and what the effects are of a piece of MaT existing. It's core to understanding how the magic and/or technology of your world exist.

Question #3: How Is It/Was It Distributed

MaT solves problems, and is thus desirable. This means people are going to want to get their hands on it, make sure others have it, ensure access. How it's passed on is extremely important as that affects who has it, who can use it – and how it can be found or lost.

Is there hidden technology or are spells publicly available? Are there famous professors and engineers, or are secrets passed on in darkened rooms among a select few? The dissemination of MaT affects how it gets to people, how those people are treated, and how people react to it. It also affects how long a piece of MaT endures. If important inventions aren't disseminated they may be forgotten, while less impressive creations remain.

In answering this question, it's important to ask how information flows in your settings. If everyone is literate, written plans/spells/etc. can spread easily. If a secret psychic technique can only be learned telepathically, then it might be a bit harder to pass around.

Of course, this is also where culture plays a big part in understanding how MaT works in your world.

Question #4: Who Can Use It?
You have MaT. You have a solution to a problem. Who can use it?

A magical discipline may only work for a limited set of people. Social mores may prevent a technology being passed around. Horrible side effects of a strange spell may mean only a few suicidally brave souls even use it. Culture, ecology, biology, and more come together to make the use of MaT very complicated – or very easy.

This requires you think about a lot of elements in your setting, from culture to inherent limitations and advantages of the intelligent species in your setting. But then again, that's part of worldbuilding.

Question #5: What's The Cost?
Nothing comes without a price. If you're lucky, it's just a price you don't mind paying. That's a core part of Magic and Technology.

MaT may require resources, time, discipline to use. There may be upkeep, from repairing a device to retaining psychic discipline. Teachers have to be paid, smuggled technology requires untraceable currency to buy, and the Wood Wizards of Arborath won't appreciate someone dealing their spells. You don't get something for nothing.

The cost of MaT is going to factor into how characters use it, economic impacts, cultural attitudes, and even ecologies. What happens when your sorcerer discovers spells produce toxic waste magic – let alone our own confrontations with the impact of modern technology.

In fact, this can be a core of many a tale in your world.

Question #6: How Is It Regarded?

Not all magic or technology is equally well-regarded, appreciated, or doing its job People like one thing and dislike another. Forms of MaT may fall out of favor for various reasons – some good, some not.

In designing your world, remember that MaT is something people have opinions on and cultures develop rules around.

Such regard and opinions aren't necessarily rational. A spell that can save the day may not be used because some supposedly evil wizard invented it. A great technology may be used as the inventor was famous, but it can turn out his creation is terribly flawed.

Asking what people think about MaT and specific elements of it in your setting is important.

Question #7: How Has And Will It Change?

MaT changes. Technology isn't static. People find new ways to use spells ("I'll throw the cloudburst spell inside his helmet"). Technology is repurposed to work better. Humans like to tinker, and my guess is most intelligent life probably would as well.

So MaT is going to change in your setting from need, from accident, and of course people wondering "what happens when I do *this*?"

Are people trying to improve the MaT they have? Apply it in new ways? What are the results and repercussions? What are the social implications of these attempts to improve? What do these improvements cost in time, money, accidents, etc.?

You may find your world isn't as static as you seem – but that's part of the fun.

Closing

Writing MaT takes effort. Spells and starships are not dead things or plot devices (at least, not when done well) but a vital part of your world and the lives of your characters. There are repercussions to every invention and every conjuration, and things are always changing.

But when you ask the right questions and think ahead, then your world comes to life even more, and because MaT is used to change that world, it may get very interesting story-wise.

The more you introduce, the more the technology differs from what you know, the more work you'll have ahead of you. However, that also means a richer, more detailed, and more believable world.

The Differences Between Magic And Technology

Last section, I looked at writing magic and technology for your setting and noted that they are essentially the same in worldbuilding: they're how you affect the world. I still believe that, but I'd be remiss if I didn't call out the differences as well. Or perhaps I should say "areas of variance," as it gets complicated.

I believe it's important to look at these differences, as in too many cases creating the magic and/or technology for a setting treats them as the same for all the *wrong* reasons as opposed to the right ones. Technology easily becomes hand-woven neutron particle miracle rays, a mythology with lab tools and circuit boards. Magic can get systematized or explained in such a way it either is technology, or is really just magic wearing technology's clothes and wandering around looking a bit lost.

There are also cultural and genre expectations of your readers or people playing your game or whatever media it is you create. There are some expected differences in magic and technology, and you'll need to consider them to make a world believable. You will also need to consider them if you want to pull the rug out from underneath your audience.

So, having suggested that you have to look at them as similar for the sake of worldbuilding, I now want to deal with when you have to look at them differently. Yes, this may produce writing whiplash, but who said worldbuilding was going to be boring and straightforward? I certainly didn't promise that.

Think of it as general and specifics. In general, Magic and Technology are the same in that they're the ways people change and affect the world. In specifics, well . . .

The Magic-Technology Continuum

When it comes to writing magic and technology, think of them as a continuum. On one end is pure magic where the laws we know in real life don't really matter or exist, and on the other is essentially fiction so realistic it comes with a bibliography and a list of reference papers. Most writing is somewhere in that wide, wide area in the middle, though usually nearer one end or another.

It's important to know where your world stands on this continuum. If you're writing a scientific thriller, you'd better be doing your research. If you're writing a magical world, you may screw it up by giving us sixteen pages of systematic description that sounds like an engineering manual with runes and potions. If you're doing Space Opera it's a bit more muddled, with recognizable technology that often serves to get things to happen, much as doing a steampunk magical world wanders in the middle ground happily with "imaginary science."

In turn, your world will vary greatly in several factors. In fact, for the rest of this section I'm going to call out these factors to note how magic and technology differ. These are not just ways "more science" and "more magical" worlds vary, but are areas your world will vary in *despite how you defined them*.

A magical world with alchemy may have it's "scientific" elements, and an SF world with psychic powers is going to verge into magical territory. In a few cases, a setting really is just cosplaying as another or is meant to ape another, such as post-apocalyptic stories with a fantasy feel. Sometimes Magic or Technology is a viewpoint (which you know if you ever tried to explain to the technologically-uninformed), which could lend all sorts of richness to your worldbuilding.

Easy? Not always. But the challenge is worth it, and let's face it, most writers just can't stop anyway . . .

Magic And Technology: The Differences

So let's look at where magic and technology differ. For your setting, you'll not only want to read the summarizes below, but ask if they fit your world. Think of them not just as important areas of difference to consider, but questions to ask!

By the way, if you look at technology and note at some point it seems almost magical, then I'll refer you to Sir Clarke and my previous corollary.

Accessibility

How available is the magic/technology/whatever of your universe? How do people get a hold of it?

- **Technology:** Is usually more accessible in settings. Not being of an "outside" origin or needing a living channeler, it can be taught, expounded on, and created to some extent by anyone with the tools and training. It also is something that is bound by known laws, so it is not odd or strange unless intentionally so, so people can usually understand it easier.
- **Magic:** Magic is usually mysterious and inaccessible, limited by rules that are not always of the material world, and not always accessible. In a few cases, because it is so powerful and such a force outside the normal world, it's also very dangerous for the effect it has on the normal world.

Access also ties into . . .

Acquisition

How do you actually get a hold of your technology or magic? This affects your setting and thus the tales within it because these are resources no matter if it's due to gears or magic crystals.

- **Technology:** Technology is usually acquired by understandable means, some as mundane as "cash or charge?" There may be little sense of wonder or thought about technology as after awhile it's unremarkable, as is getting a hold of it. It's only when innovations happen or need to happen that it may get interesting.
- **Magic:** Magic usually is harder to get a hold of because it is more mysterious, and often there's some "internal" personal element the user has to acquire, be born with, or be touched by. This is not always the case in some settings, but usually there's "something" special about the user that lets them use it, even if it's training.

Componentization

Can the components of one tool (be it magical or technical) be used or repurposed into another? Can you easily break down and build something up – or even repair via replacement?

- **Technology:** Technology can usually be broken into components. Whether it's putting a new head on an old spear or swapping out carburetors, technology is all about components. It's the ability to make regular components that allowed our mass production age, and we humans do like the convenience of standardization.
- **Magic:** Magic is rarely componentizable. It may require components to produce certain effects or items, but it's rare in portrayals of magic to break it down again. You don't often see a wizard field stripping a spell and then giving it some new runes for an awesome extra flashy effect (though that is an amusing idea).

Evolution

How does technology or magic improve? The two tend to differ in that it's assumed technology is improved upon over time, while with magic it gets fuzzier.

- **Technology:** Technology usually is developed and improved over time, and that may be a driving element of a world. It's development is often driven by its users, or if it achieves sentience, itself.
- **Magic:** Magic usually does not evolve or improve, or improves slowly or based on outside forces. There's no hard and fast rule with magic, but I usually find magical settings do not have so much evolution as research, uncovering, or unleashing of power. Rarely is there anything new under the sun.

Independence

Does the technology exist and function independent of it's user/wielder? Can anyone just pick it up or is it more personal/personally bound?

- **Technology:** Technology is usually impersonal unless specifically designed to be personal. Someone can pick up a gun and fire it, ride a bicycle, and so on. If a piece of technology needs knowledge to use, that knowledge can be acquired. Personalized technology or technology keyed to a certain individual exists, but that can often be cracked, transferred, and overridden. The personal is *intentional*.
- **Magic:** Magic is often personal; in fact, a major defining feature of magic seems to be you literally need a living/sentient being to do it (apologies to all Litches and so forth). The living wielder is a necessity, and often the magical use is very personal – learned, practiced, and part of the magician. This does change in the case of artifacts, but often those are highly personalized (just ask King Arthur).

Production

How is it made? These important artifacts/spells/abilities have to come into being somehow, even if someone's born with it because they were the seventh son of a seventh son.

- **Technology:** Technology is usually manufactured by a mixture of skill, knowledge, and mechanization. The element of mechanization, where technology makes technology, is a strong element of a lot of worldbuilding. Technology's ability to improve itself is a major difference from most ideas of magic. This also leads technology to be, in many cases, kind of impersonal.
- **Magic:** Magic is usually something relatively organic (magical energy in a living being, divine power), and often eternal (spirits of ancient days, old wisdom). Magic is often not so much produced as researched almost like it is extracted from the universe. However, when you get to artifacts and items, you're entering more into a form of production. Those often have unique, almost personal origins, such as a sword made from the bones of a dead god.

Rules

Everything has rules. We humans think in rules. But rules for Technology and Magic tend to be a bit different.

- **Technology:** Technology's rules are also the rules of the everyday world. Your car and your pencil are of the same atoms, and the laws of fluid dynamics define both rivers and your bloodstream. Technology's rules tend to be omnipresent, even if they get a mite funky in (and outright flaky in the abuse of) quantum physics.
- **Magic:** Magic has rules, but in many cases they are rules that don't run like those of the everyday world, even if they work within them. In some cases this is just the way it is; in other cases magic comes from an other reality or a super-reality. Magic's rules and the world it is used in may be radically different, which may be a major theme of your setting.

Closing

Magic and Technology are often the same from a worldbuilding standpoint as noted earlier, but when you get into defining them then there's distinct, if often fuzzy differences. Looking these over, asking questions, helps you better know what you're aiming for, what you've created, and what you can create.

The Tower Of Babble-On: Technology, Magic, And Language

When worldbuilding technology of any kind – from spells to computers – characters have to discuss it. You discuss technology in your everyday life because it is part of everyday life. Your characters should as well.

By technology, I mean anything used to achieve a goal, be it a potion or a tank. For the sake of not having to say "technology and magic" over and over a gain, I'm going to refer to this as Technology most of the time.

The reason I don't use my past "MaT" (Magic and Technology) is that poor language usage often comes into play when it gets to Technology. Magic sometimes has terminology issues, but Technology seems to suffer the most abuse due to language So when I talk Technology here I'm referring to Magic as well, but acknowledging that Technology proper is where we *really* screw it up.

When we talk Technology, we face the most fascinating question of how people using Technology refer to it in our worlds. Think of how many words we have for tools and so forth. Think of how characters need to refer to Technology in their worlds.

Think of how we often do it wrong in making the worlds these characters are in.

A Rabble Of Babble

Technobabble is a general term used for "scientific-sounding" BS terminology used to refer to Technology. Many science fiction stories and properties are infamous for this; *Star Trek* is often joked about, but it's actually everywhere. It's that term made from throwing together three scientific terms, or that spell that sounds like something no normal human (or elf) would use to actually describe something.

You know the kind of terms I'm talking about. Terms meant to sound right that end up sounding all wrong.

I really didn't get how bad it could get until I got into making the random generators at Seventh Sanctum. I'd make ones to describe weapons and Technology, and suddenly I could see how words were just slammed together to make something vaguely technical in some fictional settings. I could see how often mystical spells in games and literature had come from The Home Of The Assembled Adjective.

There's something about Technobabble that just feels *wrong*. It's the uncanny valley of Technology, because it's got words but it doesn't feel like ones humans would use.

It's words made by an author, not a character in the setting.

That's the problem.

Diagnosing The Problem: The Forms

To discuss the best way to avoid Technobabble, I'd like to look at the problem and then step back on how to solve it. The reason for this is simply because we're too used to technobabble, and we don't always see it or see when we've created it and unleashed on the world.

We're used to fictionally crafted worlds, with their made-up terms, and of course their technobabble and magicbabble. It's something we just sort of plow through and tolerate and really promise we won't do . . . right before we do it.

Yet it keeps returning. Technobabble is kind of the shingles of bad terminology.

So the first step to addressing technobabble is to look for the warning signs.

Classic Technobabble: When you've got Heisenberg Rail Cannons and Nomydium Alloy Quantum Stabilized Armor you have straight-up classic grade A technobabble. This is when you've thrown a lot of sciencey/magical words together that really don't say much. If your terms sound like a pretentious Frankenstein's monster of words, it's technobabble.

Coldbabble: Coldbabble is technobabble's more-evil twin. This is when your description sounds like a kind of operating instructions or label when that's not appropriate. It's a spell that an actual person calls "A Level 3 Muscle Mending Spell" or a technology referred to as a "Flesh Restoration Pod." It says *something*, but not in the way most people would; I don't call my car a Personal Moving Device, for example.

Transplant Babble: This occurs when people graft terminology from one setting or one idea into another with no good reason. It's fantasy characters referring to light spells as Lasers just so the audience gets it when they wouldn't. This is a less common issue, but now and then you'll see it, and it stands out.

So how do you avoid these traps and others I doubtlessly haven't identified? It's simple.

You've got to stop naming Technology and ask what the people *in your setting* would call it.

Language As A Tool For Tools
Why do we have special terms for technology (and magic and other tools)? Simple. We need to refer to them properly.

We need to call a hammer a hammer when you just need someone to hand it to you. We may refer to a computer with more detailed description, like make or model, to communicate that information to a technician. We need to refer to tools so we can talk about them, just like anything else, but the proper form of communication depends on many factors.

The key to writing good technical language and avoiding technobabble is to ask what language is needed to refer to said tools – *in* the setting, *by* the characters, *for* a situation.

There's probably many ways to refer to a piece of Technology depending on context. The reason Technobabble of all kinds often seems weird as characters will use the same made-up terms in all situations. I don't know about you, but when I'm bleeding I ask for "the healing thing" not "The Mark Twelve Regenerative Restoration Pod."

Let's look at the factors that affect naming Technology to understand it.

Factor 1 – Context
Terminology depends on context – who is speaking, who is being spoken to, and so forth. Technology of all kinds will have terms relevant to the context it is used in.

Technology will probably have multiple names, but all should be meaningful depending on who is using them.

The pain in your leg probably has a very long Latin term your doctor uses, and it describes the symptom in a detailed way. A car engine is properly an internal combustion engine, but who curses their "internal combustion engine" for not working? We refer to an explosive called TNT, but the name is derived from the chemical formula of the explosive, trinitrotoluene. Do you want to use that long string of syllables every time?

Language to refer to Technology should:

- Fit the context of the situation.
- May have multiple ways to be referred to.
- Should communicate information.

Context drives the language in many ways. In fact, many of the following factors relate to it.

Factor 2 – Usefulness Of Terms

Language must be useful. Remember when I said that context was important and different words may apply to the same Technology? This is where it gets important.

Language to refer to things will vary with the situation. It's all well and good to go looking for a Hyperflux Restablizing Neutronium Balance Capacitor, but sometimes you just need to "find the damn capacitor." You don't want to refer to a spell as a "Gate Spell" during your final magic exam when there's twenty-two different variants of it and three of those allow the Worldrenders to enter our realm to eat the souls of the innocent.

We use different language for Technology depending on the situation. All Technology has should have ways to be referred to based on the situation itself. You really don't have time to ask for "Mordak's Third Level Incandescent Sphere of Fiery Doom" when you really want to yell "Fireball them!" as you run away from rabid kobolds.

Language to refer to Technology should:

- Be useful for appropriate situations (and likely will be due to a kind of language Darwinism).
- Be applicable to dealing with those situations.

Factor 3 – Person Or Persons

Technical terminology used will vary among the people talking. An engineer, a scientist, and a disgruntled user are going to refer to computer parts and processes in very different ways. A wizard, a priest, and a warrior may refer to spellcraft differently.

There will thus be different words used by people in a group, among people in a group, and between groups. These can be as varied as any other set of words – because people are varied.

Consider the possible influences:

- Social roles.
- Backgrounds.
- Personal attitudes (a proscribed magic or technology may be referred to insultingly).
- Slang and custom references.
- Knowledge and ignorance.

Individual characters will often have different tastes and needs for how they refer to Technology. You need to understand how the people in your setting see the different Technologies and refer to them. When their discussion can sound like the last time you and a friend tried to set up a video game set or fix a car, then you've made Technological language realistic.

Language to refer to Technology should:

- Be appropriate to the characters and their backgrounds.
- Be appropriate to the interactions of the characters as the characters feel is proper.
- Be appropriate to character needs.

Factor 4 – Time

Terminology changes. Grab one of the handy slang dictionaries available at bookstores or online, and you may be amazed what words used to mean and what phrases vanished. "Hilary" used to be a man's name. The term "mook" has had a variety of meanings. Even as you read these now, these simple references may have changed from when I wrote them.

In creating terms in your stories, ask yourself how terms may have changed over time, or how they were preserved. A tradition-bound culture may use archaic references, and a culture with a lot of immigration may adapt a rainbow of foreign words quickly. This happens to Technology as well; do we refer to cars as motorcars anymore in America?

A quick guide to see how time affects technical terms:

• Age of Technology – If Technology has been around a long time, people probably have casual ways to refer to it. If its new, there may be very few terms, and those may be quite technical.
• Importance of the original name – If it's vital for some reason that a Technology be referred to very specifically, words for it may not have changed or changed much. On the other hand if it doesn't matter, terms may change quickly, possibly to some people's frustrations. ("Junior, it's a Thunderous Bolt of Lightning, not a 'Flash and Zap'.")
• How easy was the original name to use – The goal of communications is to, well, communicate. If an important Technology is hard to refer to, people will probably come up with new, simpler words.

Language to refer to Technology should:

• Evolve with people's needs, social structure, and history.
• Exist for a practical reason – and if practical may not change that much.

The Last Word Of This Section

Technical terminology is part of language, part of the language of your setting, and thus should serve the needs of those using that language. When you keep the human (well, sentient) factor in mind, it becomes very clear why Technobabble fails.

Technobabble fails because it's unrealistic and doesn't fit the characters and world. It's when you reach in from outside and inflict language *on* your setting.

Instead, let the language for Technology come *from* your setting. It's much more realistic and believable.

Religion

Creating Religion Is Hard

Let's talk about creating and writing religions in your world. You may now start panicking if the title of this section didn't already set you off.

Creating religions is challenging, as any worldbuilder knows. That sense of challenge, the burden of doing it, the social issues involved, and the awareness of all the effort it takes can bring you down. Chances are even mentioning this is giving you unpleasant flashbacks in your worldbuilding efforts.

So before I explore writing religions and creating religions in your setting, I want to cover the challenges worldbuilders face – and discuss overcoming them. Will I cover all possible cases? No. There's only so much I can do or remember, swear to . . .

. . . er, anyway, let's go on and look a some of the challenges facing creating religion in our settings and the common obstacles we encounter.

Before I get on to "why this is so hard," let me note that I am covering religions in the somewhat more narrow theological sense, where there's at least a suggestion of metaphysics, the supernatural, and so on. This is to avoid what has happened to the word "religion" in the English language.

Actually, before we go further, let me explain why I'm so cagey on the word "religion."

I find the term "religion" in English has come to cover so much it almost gets useless. It's become a huge catch-all phrase. I can argue many forms of Confucianism, Buddhism, and occultism don't even count as religion, for instance. The word is often a trap because we've used to catch so much we're often talking about different things using the same word.

So for the sake of this and any writing to follow, I am assuming there's some metaphysical/spiritual/deific elements to your world-building, *or at least people believe there to be such.*

Now, onward and upward. Or downward, depending on your celestial or infernal inclinations.

Here's the challenges I usually see in worldbuilding and religions – and advice for you to overcome them.

Seen It Before

Sometimes I want to blame early *Dungeons and Dragons* for giving people the idea to port entire pantheons into unrelated fantasy settings. Much as the early game encouraged wholesale importing of the divine, some other fictional worlds have familiar deities. It may be understandable in the case of parody (Sir Terry Pratchett's hilarious Discworld goddesses and gods come to mind), but in too many cases a world's deities are just familiar gods and religions having a cosplay outing.

For whatever the reasons – past inspiration, laziness, whatever – one of the dangers of building original religions in a setting is that they start looking damned (or blessedly) familiar.

When a religion is just some previous set of gods given a free makeover, it's a big problem for worldbuilding:

- It's jarring to any informed reader who, when they realize your theological unoriginality, just starts seeing the actual religion you based your work on. It takes them out of the sense of there being a unique, living world and they just see other gods wearing new hats.
- It shoehorns ideas and concepts into your setting that don't fit it. Importing something whole cloth (or whole Golden Fleece) warps your setting; parts of it won't match up and work together.

- It looks lazy, and can make people not appreciate the world. Even a well-crafted world grates when there's that glaring unoriginality.

SUGGESTED SOLUTION: Honestly? Build a religion that fits the world, even if you have to get theological and metaphysical and put in the effort.

People Hating You

Much like real life, it seems people get pretty worked up about imaginary religions. Leaving aside those that may be offended by unoriginality, once you start diving into ethics, divinities, and so forth it just seems people will get annoyed *constantly*.

It's a lot like real life, except *you* can decide on the gods people hate each other over. Its just those decisions will make people hate you in your daily life.

Alas, this is unavoidable. People get attached to fiction and they get attached to religion, and they will find something to get pissed off over. They will also bring their own assumptions to bear on your creation, rather unfairly, but such is life.

SUGGESTED SOLUTION: Build a good religion that is well-written and fits your world. People may get annoyed over whatever issue they decide to freak out about that day, but at least your world will make sense. It sort of "armors you" when the world is consistent, leaving critics railing against a well-made fictional construct that works. Potential critics may realize the work done, and those looking for trouble will look foolish.

Preaching

What if you want to write your setting to explore deep-seated religious beliefs, experiences, and your own thoughts? Then it's challenging as well because, be honest, you're preaching a bit here. That's fine, if you're honest about it.

It's just that most people are *terrible* at preaching.

When creating a world and a tale focused on religious elements, we're usually at a loss for good role models. Sometimes the goal of the writing is theological exploration, but it's often done poorly. For every C.S. Lewis who could do it decently there's a lot of . . . non-C.S. Lewises.

(That's for people that actually *like* C.S. Lewis.)

People know when you're preaching, People know when you're trying to sell them a theological bill of goods. They just *know*.

Preachy worldbuilding is annoying – religious or not – because unless your audience wants that, it can seem contrived and manipulative. People don't like to be manipulated, and they balk at contrived ideas.

The road to hell is paved with good intentions, but in this case I'd switch intentions.

SUGGESTED SOLUTION: Explore, don't preach. Explore ideas, ask about repercussions, and really ask yourself questions as you build your world. People should be along for the ride, and so should you. A good piece of advice is that if your world and stories in it shock you with their conclusions at least once, you're exploring your world, and others will enjoy it.

A good story on an issue like religion should change you at the end. Good worldbuilding even moreso.

Wimping Out
The flipside of being preachy is wimping out with your theological worldbuilding.

It's too easy to make religions generic, or inoffensive, or barely present. Now if that's part of your setting, fine, but in a lot of our own lives we've probably seen religion and related components as prominent parts of people's lives. So when you wimp out on your religious worldbuilding, there's almost a gap in people's sense of your world.

Don't wimp out. It leaves you with a glorious world – and washed-out religions.

SUGGESTED SOLUTION: Remember religion is part of your world and build along with it, and keep faith (ha!) with the world you're making. Make it work, make it hang together, religion and all. If people get annoyed . . . well, see above.

Also, try to have fun with it. It makes it easier and, frankly, provides better results.

Half-(Golden) Assing It

A strange sight I've seen in religion-building is doing it *almost* all the way. You've got some really promising things there, some believable rituals, some ethics but it's not *quite* all there.

Not taking things far enough is a constant problem in any form of worldbuilding. When it comes to religion, it actually stands out quite a bit as religion and philosophy is often a big part of people's lives. When yours is half-baked, people reading or gaming in your world will notice.

I think things get half-done because of many reasons:

1) The above fears.
2) A lack of interest in religious worldbuilding and a desire to get it over with. Not everyone enjoys this.
3) A lack of knowledge about religion that means one doesn't know how far to go in their creations.

People will notice unfinished religious worldbuilding, no matter the reasons. So you'll need to follow through.

SUGGESTED SOLUTION: Don't do it half-baked. A great idea in doing religious worldbuilding is to do what you do in other areas: start asking yourself questions until you get answers about the religions you're building.

Oh Look, It's Not

Gods save us from stories where the gods are not gods. Except for *Lord of Light* and the other books and tales that actually focused on that theme. They're my exception to the rule.

In writing religion, there's a temptation to try and explain it as something else, which is great *if it's part of your world*. If not, it gets awfully lame to decide to shoehorn in an alien computer playing god or something similar. It gets tiring after awhile, and it takes some good writing chops to make it work even if it is part of your theme.

I find this happens when people want to explain their world in certain ways or prevent complications that seems unrealistic in the setting of the world. Don't fall for that.

Let the gods be gods when they need to be.

SUGGESTION: Just write the damn religion as it fits your setting.

Is It "Religion" When It's "Real"?

Be it a setting where the gods visit and put their feet up on the coffee table, to a "religion" that borders more into poetic philosophy, sometimes one of the problems in writing religion is it's so "real" it's . . . well, reality.

We get used to the idea that religions have an ineffable, mysterious about them, but in some settings that goes right out the window – and Carlefon, God of Windows, is holding it open for you. It's a bit of a poser to ask just what's real when things we don't think of as "real" actually are.

Once we start dealing with religions as "all too real," it opens up a huge amount of writing challenges. Just like the reality of faster-than-light travel changes things in an SF setting, all-too-real gods change a lot of assumptions in their setting. A lot of rules and concepts are gone when the gods can get involved.

- If prayer works, why aren't people pestering the gods all the time?
- If gods have agendas, then the real world's politics become a lot more complex.
- If the gods are intimately involved with mortals on a romantic level, what of the kids?

If you don't deal with these changes, then your setting becomes disconnected. Not dealing with the reality of gods in a fantasy setting, for instance, is as unrealistic as not dealing with nuclear weapons in a modern setting. Even distant, their presence is felt.

SUGGESTION: If religion is real in your setting, then it's real. Accept it, don't let it overwhelm you, but deal with it as a good worldbuilder. Put some time in to ask about the implications of the religious truths of your world.

Closing
Hopefully this has addressed some of the challenges and pitfalls of religious worldbuilding. Am I done yet? Nope, there's more.

Worldbuilding And Religion: General Advice

When I worldbuild, I confess building religions and so on are some of my favorite things to do. This is due to my own inclinations and interests in people, psychology, culture, and religious experiences. Not everyone shares my enthusiasm.

Fortunately, as I have such enthusiasm, I've got plenty of advice to share for those less inclined. Here's a few things I've found help in doing religious worldbuilding. Think of this as general rules to help you be better at building this complex subject.

Know Thy Subject

If you want to write about religion in your world, go get some religious knowledge.

A good worldbuilder is a bit of a renaissance person in that they should know enough diverse subjects to build their world, and to know when they are ignorant or make a mistake. Religion is just part of worldbuilding, like the plants and the cultures and the Jurmaxian Hypercube Cars. You need *some* knowledge to do it right, even if it really lets you hand-wave better.

In short, if you want to write religion, learn about religion.

You Don't Have To Be Religious; You Do Have To Relate

A good writer can get inside the head of their characters no matter how different they are. You have to relate to your character's religious attitudes and experiences even if you don't share them – you need empathy.

Sometimes people are adverse to stepping into the shoes and soul of someone with a different religious belief than them. Perhaps it's due to the complexity of the subject, or the personal differences they have. Perhaps it's simply that they find religion boring. I find religious empathy is rather difficult for people, perhaps due to the lack of it in the world.

Whatever differences between you and the people you're writing, the important thing is not that you agree with their religious beliefs, but that you understand them. It's the same for anything involving your cast, really, but religion is an area we easily fall down on empathy-wise.

How do they think? How do they feel? Why do they believe? What does it mean to them? What is it like to be them?

Developing this empathy is also excellent writing and worldbuilding practice. If you can understand someone who believes differently than you or lives in a religious environment alien to you, then you'll be far better at crafting a setting and a tale. You'll experience and understand the setting and story with an intimacy that will help you.

Some Things Are Expected – Be Aware Of Them

Some people have certain expectations of religions, gods, morals, and/or miracles. If you leave these things out, it may make your world hard to believe in. There may be good reason to leave them out, but if so you need to cover that.

Perhaps your world has gods, but without gender – which may seem strange to people used to gendered gods. "Prayer" may not exist in your setting because people walk down to the temple and talk to the god directly. Those things may seem neat – but they may seem weird to an audience with more traditional expectations.

Worldbuilding with religions requires you to navigate the expectations of those reading or gaming in your world. You might leave something out that should be there, but also risk including things that aren't appropriate because people "expect" them. You're really stuck between the Rock Of Ages and a hard place.

This is a hard issue to deal with. On one hand, the feeling "wait, I'm missing this" can be a red flag that you did miss something. On the other, it could be that you worried more about expectations than worldbuilding and distracted yourself from doing your job.

The best approach to "religious expectations" in your setting is to do the following:

- Include what fits in your setting, not the reader expectations. Focus on good worldbuilding.
- Detail your setting enough that you "know" it and it makes sense.
- When you're comfortable with your world, those moments of asking "should this go in?" will be almost immediately answered because of your in-depth knowledge.
- Don't flaunt differences between reader expectation and you world unless that's part of the point. Let them discover it.
- Rely on the well-designed setting to be something the reader can understand and answer their questions. When they go "why is this not what I expected?", their experience with the world should help them see why.

Document – Trust Me

Religion is just like anything else in your world, and you should document it like crazy. If you're not theologically inclined it's even more important as this stuff isn't going to stick in your head easily. Document, document, document.

It's too easy to make religion an afterthought when it shouldn't be, so this could help you get better at recording it. It may even let you develop some good documentation techniques or templates for your work.

Perspectives Are Important

Remember, your religion in your world is still seen and acted on by the characters in said world. Whatever you write is seen through the lenses of characters (even if they're gods and goddesses). So when you write, avoid a gods eye view – unless, of course, an actual god is involved. Even then there's no reason to assume they know everything unless they're omniscient. It's all perspective.

It can be too easy to write religion with an outsiders view, especially if said religion is "true" in the world setting. Religions are practiced by people, and treating it from an outsider view loses that. When an unsure character states a religious truth with utter conviction, or someone simply goes through a ritual that should be important yet it seems rote, you've lost something.

Forgetting perspective makes your characters and thus your world hard to believe, and yanks the audience out of a sense of immersion.

Besides, a good ol' religious disagreement is some great worldbuilding and writing, at least once the smoke clears.

Conclusion

Hopefully this has you ready to do some religious writing. If not, well there but for the grace of . . . you get the idea.

Worldbuilding With Real Religions

So you're worldbuilding, but the world is basically like ours, or like a given historical place and time. You'd start building religions, but you're dealing with real religions that people practice and live right now (or the ancestors or descendants of those religions). You're not so much creating them as asking where they fit into your setting and what you have to write.

It should be easy, right, since you're dealing with a premade religion? Not when you realize that when it comes to religion you have to . . .

- Treat as a functioning part of your setting.
- Know what you're writing about.
- Write/describe/handle it in a realistic way (or a way that seems realistic) relevant to what is real *in your setting*.
- Deal with annoying people who will not like what you've done no matter what.

So you've got to design your "real" world, but also deal with "real" religions. How do you handle these challenges?

Lets' get traditional and throw down some commandments.

The First Commandment: The Setting Is The Truth

The first thing to remember as a worldbuilder is to know the truth of your settings. Know what is real, what is false, what is appropriate, and what is left kind of fuzzy. You must know even if no one else will know or care.

Know the truth. Religion is the same way. You need to know what's really going with religion in your world, from "it's all BS" to "angels are aliens" to "eh, it's not that relevant but let's deal with the human side."

The level of depth you need may vary by what you're doing.

You may not need to go too deep. If you're doing a real-world setting and telling a tale of a "rom-com story at a computer company." You may not care about metaphysical depths, and they may not matter; the "personal" accuracy is all you need, but you should get that right.

If you dive into defining science and metaphysics, or if religion is a part of it of the real world you're building, then you're going to have to decide what's real. This may well mean deciding on religious truths and falsehoods in your setting. This means research, knowledge, and perhaps even deep speculation that may not be comfortable.

Remember, in your setting things happen for a reason. That includes religion. You decide what goes in.

WARNING: One danger of writing about real religions is that you'll bring in a lot of assumptions into your setting that may not matter, or worse may have an obvious agenda. Be careful of bringing in biases when they're not needed or are more a case of preaching than creating.

The Second Commandment: Know Thy Religion
Do not, ever, try and worldbuild or write about a "real" religion without an appropriate level of knowledge about that religion. When in doubt – any doubt – you should research it. If you do not do this research, you will be sorry.

You *will* get it wrong. You *will* embarrass yourself. You *will* piss people off and they *will* have reason. You *will* offend people in an actually understandable way. There's a very good chance you can look ignorant or even like a bigot despite good intentions. It will certainly mark you as a poor worldbuilder and yank people out of your setting.

Religion, like politics, philosophy, and good homemade chili, is about depth and personal experiences. Just think of whatever religion you were raised in and how many different variants, denominations, splinter groups, and outright cults there are.

Now amplify that by humanity. That is the potential diversity of religious attitudes and experiences you could be writing about.

If religion is any part of your work, go do some research. Much like any worldbuilding, I recommend going to the depth of "more than your reader needs to know" so you have a good sense of your world and the setting. A few bits of advice:

1) Internet research. Online calendars and a few quick articles may give you basic information and show you some surprising things.
2) Talk to people. Want to really get a feel for religion? Talk to its adherents. They may be interested in sharing.
3) Libraries, books, and more. People love writing about religion, so you can find out a lot by hitting the books. Be careful in that scholarly works can miss the "gut" elements of religion, and some religious books have an agenda.
4) Talk to non-practitioners who know what they're doing. This may include your friends or scholars.
5) Keep your own library of books on religion if it's a big deal for what you write. You'll be thankful.

WARNING: One danger of doing religious research, ironically, is you can go so far down the rabbit hole (or up Yggdrasil) that you end up over-detailing your work. This can get pretty fascinating, so know when to stop (or at least stop talking) because the reader or player in your world may not appreciate your slavish focus on detail.

The Third Commandment: Realism Is People

When putting religion in your setting, no matter what the true metaphysical elements of your writing, you are still writing about people. Yes, I'll keep noting this.

Religion in your world, be it religiously themed or where religion is a tangential detail, is about people. People who pray, meditate, doubt, believe, hope, perform rituals, give up on traditions – when you write, you write about people. When you build your world, people learn of it through the tales of those living in it.

As noted repeatedly, my philosophy is that people are the lenses through which your world is viewed. When you write, you need to get into their heads. With deep issues like love, sex, and religion, you need to get their deep seated feelings. That helps you write religion believably as you're writing them believably.

It doesn't matter what's true or false. The truth of your world is often what people think is true and false.

Whether your setting is hard-science real-world where you assume nothing metaphysical, or if an angel hides behind every scientific discovery, it's all about people in your settings and how they believe. Whether you have a God or gods in your story, the God/gods-eye view is for you, not the characters. Create them, know them, and write them as people.

This also makes stories far richer because you're writing *people*. Too often one can see discussions of religion forget the human factor. Keeping that human factor if religion plays a part in your world will make it a better because it will be believable.

Even if people disagree with their – or your – religion's viewpoints, this humanity will make the world something they can still get into.

WARNING: This "human level" understanding needs to be applied to all your major characters, otherwise some will become pastiches or parodies. The worldbuilder faces the daunting challenge of understanding the humanity of people they disagree with at best, or find abominable at worse.

The Fourth Commandment: Haters Gonna Hate, So Don't Encourage It

You will, in creating religious elements in realistic settings, annoy people. They will be miffed, they will be angry, and some may get very aggressive. Though the latter is most unlikely, you never know.

It is going to happen.

Now if you write well-done characters in a believable setting, if there's a true sense of humanity, most people will understand. Writing with empathy, will help immensely. People might get annoyed, but if your characters are human (and treated as such) that will be mitigated or even be educational.

Unfortunately, some people *like* to be annoyed and angry.

So really, all I can say is, accept it – and write so well the irrationally angry people are obviously just irrationally angry and they end up negating themselves.

On the other hand, if you go looking for it? People will oblige. So don't do it.

WARNING: Don't be casual about the possibility people may be annoyed over your handling of religion, because it may be a sign that you've actually gotten things wrong. Evaluate responses as rationally as possible, since there are opportunities to learn.

So Why Do All This?

So why spend your time researching and empathizing, and all that especially when religion is a bit of a minefield?

To be a good worldbuilder.

All of this is about the integrity of you as a creator, as a writer/designer or however you use the world, and doing a good job. This is just par for the course.

The issues of writing religion only come up because it's such big deal for people, involving so many issues. But for you the big issue first and foremost is doing it right.

It may even be educational to have that clear perspective. Trust me.

Creating Original Religions

So after the last section on writing real/realistic religions, writing your own probably seems like a piece of cake, or at least a nice, easy communion wafer.

I'm not going to say it's easier. I'm going to say it's *different*.

When you write using known religions you need to do research, think over if you'll annoy people, and in general reconcile things with your setting. The challenges are the challenges of research and navigation.

Then there's creating your own religion, which pretty much puts you in the driver's seat sans God being your co-pilot.

Want to play God? You get to do more than that - you play God *about* playing God when you build your own religions.

The Core Truth Of Building Your Own Religions

When you're designing religions from scratch for your setting, it can be a daunting challenge. Rituals and beliefs, reasons and origins, happenings and habits are all your responsibility. If you've ever had any religious or theological education, ever seen a mandala diagram, or ever read a catechism, you have to world build that several times over.

Except, of course, it's not as challenging as you may think. You're already doing it.

If you're building a setting, designing characters, or making cultures and history, you're doing the heavy lifting that's no different than creating religions. In fact, it's virtually the same thing.

Religion Is Part Of Your Setting

Religions exist for a reason; a little research into any religious history of our world will tell you this. You'll find traditions that seem to be more about social cohesion than belief, religions forged from rebellion against the times, and individuals who engaged in massive mental and metaphysical explorations. There is always a reason someone stood up as a prophet or went and meditated in a cave.

If you're building a setting, you're already building the groundwork for your religion. You know the metaphysics, the culture, if there are gods or just space aliens playing a prank, the source of magic, and so on. You already know your world.

So really, religion is just part of the work. Religion is a very human (or sort-of-human) way of dealing with the world . . .

Religion Is A Tool

As noted, religions exist for a reason in our world, and the same will hold for your own setting. Religions should evolve naturally in your setting. Maybe, in some settings, nothing that we would call religion has been created. There may be a reason for that.

Religion exists contiguously with all of your setting, whether the gods and metaphysical forces are real or not.

Here's a few reason for religion, in the common sense, to exist:

- The gods are actually real. Kind of goes without saying that you want a way to keep up with them.
- As a proto-science. Metaphysics aside, religions really are just a way to make sense of the world.
- As a method of social control. If you can convince people some powerful being is on your side or something, it becomes a tool to control people.

- As a method of rebellion. A new ideology or new leader, with supernatural powers or powerful insights, can change the world.
- As a tradition that's empty. People may not believe in the metaphysics, but in a tradition lives on.
- As a forgotten truth. The cargo-cult reason – sometimes religion exists as a memory, long mutated, of an original article.

Religion has a reason to exist. If some of your setting's beliefs and rituals and the like make you wonder "is that really religion?" that's not a bad thing. It means you're thinking.

Religion Is About People

Religion is practiced by people. They are the reason it exists. Either they need a way to honor real gods, or a way to rebel against false ones, or whatever. They have their reasons and their practices and their goals and their issues.

Therefore, in all your worldbuilding, remember that people are the ones handling the commandments, the rituals, the inquisitions, the charities, and so on. It'll all be about people, so ask what it means to them, how they feel, what they think, how they mess up, etc.

This not only lets you write with a good sense of empathy and create good "lenses" on the world in the forms of characters, but it also lets you address the human side of religion in a believable way.

Religions Change

Religions change because people do. People practice religion, people change, society changes, and thus religion changes.

This may mean the gods are not happy about these changes (or are thrilled their subjects finally got it right), or that people like it, but it changes. If you've ever seen an argument over the latest pronouncements of a Pope, or debates over religious writings ages old, you get the idea. Religion changes – happiness with that change is another thing.

But there is always change.

In fact, there's a chance a religion may become something that's not a religion. Just think how many people practice secular versions of what was once religious holidays. A religion can evolve right out of being a religion.

(Or in a setting where the gods are all too real, a non-religious element could become religious . . . there's a tale for you).

Religions Have History

If you are any form of theologian or historian, you know a person could spend a lifetime studying the history of one religion or one religious denomination.

Because religions change, they have a past, present – and a future. There is detail and documents, debates and wars. The story of a religion can be fascinating. When you add up all the religions in a setting, you have quite a set of tales.

So when creating religions in your setting be sure to figure out their history. It's not only important to being realistic, but again, religion is not separate form anything else in our world. It interacts with the world, the world interacts with it, and things happen. The history helps you find that, build it, and be aware of it.

Some religion may be built on a mighty rock, but too much is built upon the shifting sands of time.

The Ultimate Lesson – Again

Religion is part of your setting. Not above, not below, not separate, it is as much a part of the setting as the history and physics. It's not separate.

Worldbuild it that way.

When you accept this, then the pressure is off. It's part of your setting, and you can just run with it and have fun with it and stress over it like anything else. It's really quite refreshing to just go "yeah, let's do this thing."

I also find that when you do this, it can be felt in your world. People just somehow know you took the time to explore religious elements properly instead of ignoring it or faking it.

So go make that religion.

Or lack of religion. Hey, who am I to judge?

Sex

Sex: The Biological Imperative

Let's talk about sex and worldbuilding. If you think is going to be exciting and arousing, this probably indicates you're *really* into worldbuilding. Otherwise, sex isn't exactly that enticing when you're designing it.

Sex is like air, and not in that it's part of life and sometimes involves wearing a mask. It's because sex is so omnipresent that we can miss out how important it is. We're used to it, and we take it for granted; so even though we may think about it a lot, we don't necessarily *think* about it.

This is because sex is a vital part of being human. We get used to it like we do seeing and smelling and touching. That means we can miss its complexities, and that means we miss it when creating our complex worlds. When you don't address how the characters in your setting were born so there can *be* characters in your setting, your world is the poorer for it.

Even if you never delve much into sexuality in your settings and stories, it's certainly there in the background – or it might be in the foreground and you don't know it. It's kind of like religion and technology (and may involve both of those); we get used to talking about it, but then take it for granted and don't *create* it when we build our settings.

So, let's get down to the nitty-gritty of sex and worldbuilding: the biology of the creatures in your world that are actually reproducing. In this case, I'm going to focus on sex with an inclination towards sentient species, but most of this advice is good for the development of any sexual species.

First, let's remember what sex is *for*.

The Purpose Of Sex
Sex is about information.

Living creatures are complex things – think of them as consisting of information. Due to combinations of chemicals, coded neural signals, biochemical reactions, and the like, they go on living. A look at DNA or at the complexities of memory will certainly remind you of how much we humans consist of information.

In the case of reproduction (which I shall refer to as "sex" even if it covers less exciting subjects such as reproduction by fission), progenitors are able to transmit information about themselves in a way that allows it to be used to create new life. Semen and eggs, spores, whatever are all ways to transmit information.

In the case of humans, the DNA of the parents provides the blueprint for a new person to develop in the body of one of the partners. No matter what kind of creatures you build, sex comes down to information being used to create new life. Even simple cellular division involves "spinning off" something that has the information to keep living processes going.

In the case of more complicated reproduction, like human sexuality where DNA combines, it goes beyond transmission. Something unique and new can be born from two people combining their genetic information, making sex like a conversation.

(In the case of solo reproduction, it may be more of a rhetorical conversation.)

When you start thinking about the biology of sex in your setting, always remember it comes down to information being transmitted and being allowed to form new life.

However, *all* life is about information. It's locating food or holding a rally that leads a country to victory in a war. It's about smelling out a predator or about listening for the right tone to tell you your significant other is cheesed off. Life is input and output and retention and processing of information.

All of this information processing, sensing, thinking doesn't have specific boundaries in complex living creatures (at least the ones we observe). Smell can help one find a mate or identify poison. A person's rage may lead them to a fight out of anger, or to win through to protect the children they love. All the information that makes up a creature, wants and needs and memories and senses, is a complex web where nothing is truly "one thing."

That includes sex, the most primal method of dealing with information. Sex gets complicated in complex creatures like, well, us.

Think how much sex affects all the other parts of our life as creatures of information. It ties into desire and bonding, childrearing and familial instincts, boundaries and territories. That relatively simple part of our lives colors everything – and is colored by other things.

Thus, even from biological points of view, worldbuilding about sex becomes complicated because it's at the core of a living being and because its likely to touch on far more than simple reproduction. Sex sort of gets into everything.

As soon as you start addressing sex in detail in your setting, it becomes a lot more complicated. Sex is never simple. As I go on through this section, I'll touch on how sex affects all aspects of a being (or most likely does).

144 | Steven Savage

In the end, I find that when writing about sex and designing its point in your world it keeps coming back to these lessons:

- Living creatures propagate themselves. At the core a species is about transmission of information.
- Living creatures lack boundaries among their component biologies, which is understandable. That ability to suss out bad food means it's easier to give a potential mate a non-fatal gift.
- Because of this, it is likely that sex for any species you may write will go beyond the boundaries of reproduction and into all aspects of life.
- This in many ways makes sense as, again, sex is a form of communication/transmission and that is what life is about.

Now with that being said, let's move on to the three basic kinds of sexuality you may end up designing in your worlds. We'll get into the even more complex elements later in following sections, but I want you primed for things to get complicated.

Situation Normal

If you're writing about people that are, for all extents and purposes, human, it may seem pretty easy to write about sex and ignore it all together. It's just standard. It's normal. It's background noise, though perhaps with an uninspired soundtrack.

This is where things tend to go wrong because we don't pay attention. It's too easy to just figure "oh this is just a bunch of people like us" and then not think about sex and your world. This ignores how complex sex is for human beings.

Consider all the biological sexual issues that we humans face:

- Issues of contraception.
- Issues of social diseases.
- The duration of pregnancy.

• Complications of pregnancy.
• Biological issues due to sex organs, from ovarian cysts to enlarged prostates.
• Biological transformations such as puberty and menopause and their side effects.

If you're going to do any kind of setting with regular people, the biology of sex is likely to come up, even if it's just figuring someone hauls off and kicks another character in the junk and it hurts. Sex may be a minor issue, but it's almost certainly there.

In most cases, writing "humans like us" and sex really focuses not on the biology (with which we have passing familiarity), but psychology and culture. That may lull you into a false sense of security because then you can just throw a few common ideas in without thinking about the squishy bits.

So when worldbuilding "normal" humans, take a moment to inventory any issues of sex that may come up. A quick list is:

• What diseases exist that are sexually transmitted or involved? This will also affect culture and medicine.
• What areas of sexual transformation are affected by the setting? For instance, in an era of malnutrition, puberty and pregnancy will be adversely affected.
• What other environmental or setting factors may affect sexuality? This can radically affect your setting. If a virus is causing sterility in your setting, you need to design it to explain why there is a population left in your setting.
• How do cultural and psychological and even metaphysical elements affect sexuality – attitude, access to contraception, and so on? Biology is a powerful thing, but these other factors will affect it.

Even in writing a real-world setting, don't always assume you know enough about sexual biology to write. A little research is in order if it's remotely part of your story. Because of many issues (both psychological and cultural), you may know less than you think.

Perhaps you're writing beings that aren't essentially human. That's a bit more complex – and all these various issues of puberty and contraception still exist for them as well. When you get to the not-quite humans, worldbuilding sex gets even more challenging.

Sex And The Possibly Single Almost-Human

Then you get into settings or setting elements where you have almost-humans. Your standard fantasy species, the thing-on-the-forehead-but-human-otherwise aliens, and so on. You know, the beings in the setting that are are for most intent human but a bit different.

It's often tempting in dealing with almost-humans to do two things:

- To make their sexuality just like humans, which is a bit unbelievable because they're still somewhat alien.
- To throw in a twist or something extra, but treat them just like humans despite whatever variant you threw in.

Both approaches are a mistake.

To make an almost-but-not-quite human species just like humans is to ignore all the biological differences that may be there. Even small differences can have radical effects on something as important as sex. To treat such a species as totally like humans is to toss away all your work about what's different when it comes to sex. When you do, the species doesn't seem quite right and it becomes a disjointed pile of ideas.

To throw in a twist, such as "they reproduce in half the time as humans" and then ignore it is to consciously make the choice to ignore what it means. Any change in sexuality will have a radical impact since sex is how the species comes to be.

Imagine a human-like people where the gestation period was half the time. This completely changes the effect it'd have on the role of women. Lower the sex drive of a species and it might limit their spread (as often seems to be a trope of fantasy dwarves thanks to Tolkien). A few minor changes to your "almost human" species and you have major repercussions to deal with.

In handling the biology of near-human species, I find a good way to deal with it is to stop thinking of them as near-human and focus on them as different species that has familiar elements. These familiar elements provide you a lot of useful reference points, and from there you can extrapolate on what the differences mean.

A few examples to get you thinking about your almost-but-not quite humans. What if . . .

• Your species has increased fertility due to a hostile environment? In turn, as a species tames its world, population growth may be a problem quicker. There's something to deal with in your story. "Y'know, I'm thinking our ability to have five kids at a time is starting to backfire, Becky."
• Perhaps a species has limited gestation periods. That would affect the role of whatever gender(s) carries the child as they would be less limited. "That pregnancy was the longest two months of my life – how long is it for you humans?"
• Maybe a species doesn't require someone to carry the child. Imagine humanlike beings who lay eggs. What does that mean for society, reproduction, and childrearing? "I play classical music to the egg, I hear it helps the child learn in the shell!"

- What if species have no case of menopause or reproductive limits in their lifespan? If couples can easily have children until death it changes ideal ages for marrying and conceiving. "I love my tenth son, but he's got to stop calling me grandpa, it isn't funny . . ."

Remember, you are creating a *different* species when you make human-alikes. When things get different from regular humans to any degree, you're really just designing a completely new species with a lot in common with humans. Maybe you just want to start anew.

It might be easier for people to relate to almost-humans, but they're still different.

And as noted, all that past stuff about culture and basic sexuality you face in "pretty much humans" still applies, so start asking what social disease you can catch when your species lays eggs.

Loving The Alien: The Sexual Biology Of Non-Humans

This is where it gets complicated: creating a totally new species in your setting and dealing with their sexuality.

In designing a species from scratch, you're going to enter into a very complex world. You're designing a completely separate species. That's complex enough as it is. Now you've got to ask how it reproduces.

Just think how complex sex is for humans, biologically. Now inventory all the non-human species you know about and think about *their* sexual biology. Now realize you've got to create something like that. It's enough to make you lose interest in sex of any kind.

Welcome to the cold shower of worldbuilding original species.

If you're going to populate your world with definite non-humans it's going to require you to take time, think, and do research. You're going to have to put in a great deal of effort and possibly some reading if you're going hard science.

Someone could probably write an entire book on creating sexuality of fictional non-human species. This book is more general, so instead I'm going to give you some basic advice to get you started.

- Remember that sex is about transmission and propagation, but it is likely to tie into other elements of any species, as noted earlier. Whatever the method of reproduction, it will color all other aspects of that species as reproduction is vital to having a species.
- Read up on the sexual biology of other creatures, the more unusual the better, and note how they work. It'll give you ideas, and in some cases probably horrify you beyond words.
- Determine how far you have to go. Building realistic species (or building species realistically) can be very addictive and you can go pretty far down any rabbit hole of biology, be it sex or something else.

The key to designing good sexual biology is, like many things, to know how much you have to do then take it a little farther to make sure you know enough.

I'll just have to leave it up to you if you need to get to first base or third base with sexual design. No, I can't resist these jokes.

Sex Is Important
Hope I haven't scared you off, but sex is a complicated issue, as we all know, however it's incredibly important to do in your worldbuilding.

It's a part of our own lives so readers will notice its absence.

It's part of life itself.

It might just be one of your biggest challenge as a worldbuilder. But if you're able to tackle it, you'll be rewarded with a very believable world. You'll also be rewarded with stories and games that truly take readers into new settings and let them see things differently. In thinking sex over carefully and making it believable, you'll make them think and believe in your world.

Of course once we talk biology, we have to talk about psychology, and that's next . . .

Sex: All In Your Mind

We've covered the biology of sex, which, if I did my job, should have proved to be completely unarousing unless you have a major science fetish. If you do, then you're welcome, but you owe me dinner.

The thing with creating and understanding the sexuality of the beings and creatures in your world, is that it goes beyond basic biology. Biology is just the foundation.

Sexually reproducing creatures don't just reproduce, they have to survive, interact with their environment, and *then* reproduce. In short, they have to think about sex. If sex isn't part of their minds, they aren't going to be having much of it.

Animals think about sex. You, being a human being probably think about sex. For many of us, sex seems to be a large part of our minds, to judge by random internet surfing.

This shouldn't be a surprise at all. When you've go the biology to reproduce, you need to make sure creatures actually use it to stick around. They have to think about sex.

Biology Leads To Psychology

Sentient creatures exist because of how the biology of their species brings them into being. In turn, that ability to reproduce, the inclinations and the drives will have to be part of their psychology to get them to do it all over again. Part of any creature's mind will have to be focused on reproduction so they actually reproduce.

This is when you have to ask how the biology of reproduction affects the species and characters of the world, be they in a "human normal" setting, an "animal normal" setting, or set with some completely alien set of lifeforms.

To make it easier to design your world, your species, and the sex that makes sure you have species to write about, let's look at how sex influences the mind. This is, of course, derived from my own experience as a human, but that is all I have to go with.

Research-wise, you gotta love the one you're with. So what do we have to consider in the psychology of sex in our world?

The Drive

As I noted, sex in a way is a form of communication – transmitting information so a new life form can exist. To get living creatures to have sex, and thus propagate, there needs to be something pushing them to transmit in the first place. You need an urge.

You need a sex drive.

Sex drive is a *huge* part of human psychology, as you'll know by walking through a book store for five minutes, surfing the internet for one minute, or checking your spam filter. It colors our perceptions and it affects our moods. Sex is always there, even when we pretend it's not – which many people do with great failure.

That raw drive has inspired us and made us do stupid things. Every romance story, every politician who can't keep his pants on, is a testimony to that basic drive that's inseparable from most of us. That drive also has kept us going as a species to make sure you're here reading this.

Down deep, when you build a species or even think of a human character you have to ask what their sex drive is like. What's the raw, core emotion that gets them to engage in sex, even if it's unwise?

Exercise: Ask yourself when, in the last week, sex and your sex drive influenced your decisions and activities. If you tend towards asexuality, ask about people you know.

The Connection
In the case of humans, we kind of need other people to reproduce with. To have something akin to sexual reproduction of any kind there needs to be a way to have the different organisms get together to make other organisms. There needs to be some social psychology to sex, even if the species, say, lays parasites in the skin of hosts.

Think about how much of human reproduction is the giving, receiving, and translation of signals. You signal you're interested in someone, or warn someone off. Someone signals they're ready for sex or preemptively let's others know they're not in the mood There's always communication.

After all, sex is a form of communication. When it requires someone else do it with, there's even more communication involved – and you can bet a lot of that communication is going to be part of a creature's very biology.

Some communication about sex has to be hard-coded into a creature's biology so they have something to work with. You'll have to figure out what signals are embedded within the species' psyche. No matter how advanced a civilization, no matter how low the animal, the beings in question will have some some basic drive to get them to reproduce, even if its an ancient evolutionary remnant.

A simple read up on animal mating habits and displays will reveal a dizzying array of communicating strategies in different species.

When you are dealing with sex in your world, you have to deal with communication in the species you design. What basic communication strategies do your species have to keep the species going?

Exercise: Reflect on human communication about sex and sexuality. How much of it is likely ingrained or near hard-coded, such as expressions and body language.

Exercise: If sex is a form of communication, and it requires communication, is there a difference or are they actually inseparable? What do you think?

Beyond The Moment

Children don't spring forth fully formed in humans, and I'd say there's a good chance they don't in any species you design (but if so, get crazy). Gestation period aren't instantaneous in our world, and are unlikely to be so in yours (but again, if so, enjoy). The contact of sex and the starting of reproduction is just the beginning of even *more* issues.

Think of the psychological effects of pregnancy, of the parental urges people have (or don't have in some cases), or the reaction of someone to a cute newborn. Consider the pain of childbirth, or the issues of mourning a lost child (the flipside of the parental urge). How much of this in humans is hardwired and not related to sex or courtship?

In humans, sex in the whole involves a whole lot of other behaviors, of childrearing and birthing and age. There's hormone changes and complicated desires. There's emotions and feelings and other drives.

Humanity has an entire emotional *infrastructure* for reproduction and family and childbearing that goes beyond the moment of reproduction. Otherwise, again, we wouldn't be here.

Any species you design, sentient or not, is going to have some additional emotional infrastructure surrounding sex to deal with the results, from pair-bonding (or whatever form of bonding) to childrearing. After all, any species that manages to reproduce has to follow up on actually having offspring.

When worldbuilding about sex, you really need to consider all the psychological/psychobiological elements of all that sex entails, from courtship to having children.

Sex is not the end of the biological urges and behaviors a species has. It's the beginning. As a worldbuilder, you have to consider how your species handle pregnancy if they have it, parental urges, age, and so on.

Exercise: What behaviors do you witness in people regarding "post-sex" behaviors such as childrearing, family, etc.?

Exercise: Where does "sex" end and something else begin for humans? Can you separate them?

Sex Is Everywhere

Finally, because sex is a big part of being a living creature, it tends to become part of what we are. We just may not notice it. When you get to complex sentient creatures, just think how far sex may become part of their lives.

Examine the human world and sex is everywhere It's the hydrogen of human existence, the most common element. From pornography to wedding advisors, from the latest sexy makeup to a cologne, from childrearing advice to contraception – sex is omnipresent, or is at least the inducer of many of our cultures and behaviors.

Sex also blends into other things in our lives. A sterile couple may turn their parental urges to charity, as may someone whose children have moved out. The reproductive urge blends into our sense of family and culture. How may writers or artists channel love or desire into something deep? How passionately may someone embrace an idea like a mistress or lover?

At least in the case of humans it seems we can repurpose our sex drive. If you've ever been in love with an idea or a song, you know there's a point where human love and desire can even be for something abstract.

I think this is to be expected in most sentient creatures as reproduction kind of transcends the physical act. Sex is so fused with our lives it can become more than sex.

Or maybe everything *is* sex.

Exercise: think over how many times we use sexual words for non-sexual things or things related to sex. We "love" an idea. A book "is our child." List as many as you can think of.

Exercise: what ideas, concepts, or activities do you feel true passion for? How close is that passion to love/desire/sex?

It's A Continuity
Biology leads to psychology when it comes to sex, since in a way sex is what life is about – information moving on. It's hard to separate the two.

But also in sentient creatures (well humans which we know of) sex tends to connect into so much else. In humans it influences even non-reproductive behaviors, our terms, and our feelings.

Sexuality will probably infuse the minds of any sentient species you develop to a greater or lesser extent, just as any biological element will have a wide influence. You'll want to consider all the psychological angles when you design a species.

Of course that will influence culture, and that's coming up.

Sex: Let's Get Social

So you've got sexually reproducing beings in your setting. You've worked on their psychologies and understand just how sex affects them.

In turn, you've thought about how sex affects the basic, hardwired (or at least hard-inclined) psychology of whatever species you're designing. Where you bring together two more more beings with some mutual goals and drives, the creatures have to get along and work together to survive – and thus reproduce. Once you have sex, you eventually have a crowd and they're going to need to work together.

Working together benefits everyone. You need some level of cooperation among a species to A) reproduce and B) not kill each other off. A species that is sexual, and thus social, will either develop a society or not get very far.

Be it a pack level behavior or a human-like capacity to hyperadapt and run culture as if it was a program, sex leads to social behavior. In turn that behavior is going to affect sex. Sex brings creatures into being, shapes the behaviors so they reproduce, and then there's enough of them they have to get social and you have to ask what instincts and behaviors that entails.

What can I say? Sex makes things complicated. But you knew that.

A Quick Note

I'm going to be talking social behaviors here, and I'll be referring to this as society, since you're probably focusing on sentients. However, a good chunk of this applies to less-sentient, animal-level behavior that has social behavior even if it's not a society as we think about it. Choosing one word is just easier.

In short, I'm using the word society in the broadest sense.

So What Is Society?

Let's ask: just what does a society and social behavior do for creatures who reproduce?

Society is how social living organisms arrange themselves and communicate among themselves. No man is an island, and a creature living on its own is probably dead in the end. But a society allows for members to interact, survive, and prosper – and, of course, have sex.

When it comes to sex, society lets beings hook up, reproduce, and carry on the line – and, ultimately the society. You can't separate the two if you think about it. Society lets you reproduce and deal with the results of reproduction easier, and in turn shapes those that become part of society due to that reproduction.

Society is inevitable. It is sort of the "next level" of psychology for a species. It's that principle that lets them get organized, communicate, and pass on information and genes. Thus it comes back to sex, because sex is why there are beings around to have a society in the first place.

Complex sexual creatures will have some social instincts, psychology, and other instinctive core traits. The ability to bond and socialize, both social behaviors, allows creatures to further grow and survive. Highly social creatures are almost an organism all their own, each being a cell, moving forward, growing, and surviving even as some cells are born and die.

Society itself really is about the transmission of information. Behaviors, language, rituals, and training all allow for survival but are also communicated due to social abilities. An individual, be it a poet or an animal that passes on a clever hunting trick, outlives their time and perhaps even their progeny by passing information along.

Society is almost a "second level" of sex. An individual can have vast influence beyond their individual reproduction, and their ideas, concepts, or even simple learned behaviors can echo for ages in descendants yet unborn. Someone can have no children but live on in a book or in an act.

As I said, living beings are all about communication. Sex is just the first kind. Society is sort of the next kind.

But that leaves a lot to explore, and when you talk sex and society, there's a few things you'll want to deal with concerning sex and society and issues related to it.

The Biological Level
On one level, you have to ask how much of the social instincts creatures you design are innate and how those vary.

It's very likely any reasonably complex sexual species is going to have some hardwired social instincts just so they can survive and reproduce. These may be rather basic, but are likely to extend beyond the individual psychology of raw sex drive and need. After all, if they're not hardwired enough, that drive probably isn't going to get expressed in ways that ensure good reproduction and survival.

This requires you to ask where the sexual drive, the social instincts related to sexuality, and learned social behaviors begin and end. There's the urge, the urges allowing the urge to be expressed, and then the actual society built around it.

Note that these social instincts do not always involve sex, at least directly. Sex is a big part of any living creature's behaviors (as we know), but they also have behaviors that help them survive together. Reproduction ensures members of the species exist, so

162 | Steven Savage

there are probably non-sexual or not overly sexual social drives to let them get along.

Exercise: Look at the way you spent your day today. How many things did you do that were more learned than instinctive? How many were more instinctive than learned? Who knows; when you yelled at someone for cutting you off on the freeway may have been an example of pure territorial rage.

The Developmental Level

The next thing to do in designing a species' sexual-social elements is asking what traits they have for social behavior that may be affected by sexual behavior.

Human language is a classic example of this. It's amazing that we have this ability to create symbol systems and thus pass on information. These words you are reading are in a language that evolved for eons, allowing us to employ our natural communications abilities.

However, there's not really a core "human" language, or at least not one that seems identifiable. We have the capacity for language, and that allows us to survive and interact. In turn, because we are sexual beings, a lot of language is dedicated to sex, and that language in turn is regulated by societies.

A similar example in humans is developing social roles. Though we have complex, varied societies, we still seem inclined to form social bonds and roles. It's as if we slot ourselves into them happily. Even if said role is that of an outsider, we almost need others to announce how "outsidery" we are.

Your species will have various biological inclinations that will affect societies, but also will affect sex and social aspects of it. What would natural telepathy mean for sexuality? Enhanced smell?

This is an extremely challenging area to worldbuild as you have to enter a liminal area between biological traits and the larger society beings form and ask what they're inclined to do. I find this area very rewarding to explore as you have to enter this unsure area and really ask how the life forms you designed adapt and in what parameters.

Exercise: Name five human skills/traits/abilities that you think are natural and hardwired, but are also highly developmental. What role do they play in societies in sex?

The Social Level
Ultimately, when you get to sentients or complex social beings, you end up with a society.

A society is an amazing thing. It's composed of biological creatures with some hardwired traits, who have learned various things because they're inclined to learn, and now pass the society they constructed along. Society is both something that parents its members, and these members help bring about the future of that society (to keep this whole sex thing in the picture).

At the same time, a society is a powerful thing for a species to develop. It can literally be like a unified yet adaptable organism. It vastly outlasts any of its components, it can change quickly since it's not as tied to biological components, and it can propagate information effectively. A society is the ultimate reproductive and communicative tool that can send probes to distant worlds, seed TV signals into space, and write words down that survive thousands of years later.

When you design organisms that have sex, they develop individual psychologies, they have social instincts, and ultimately they create a society.

If you think about it, this makes sense. A society is built on communication and propagating information, and because of that it allows for survival, and thus reproduction (even if it's not biological). A society is, in a way, the sophisticated triumph of sex, the primal communication. It allows the transmission of individuals and of itself.

What does this mean for the societies in your world? How does the society in your setting propagate itself? How much of that is dependent on the way your species reproduce?

Exercise: In the next five minutes, list all the ways an identifiable society is like a living organism.

Exercise: Now that you listed the similarities between a society and a living organism, list the differences.

The Social-Sexual Level
Now, back to sex.

Sex is hardwired into beings that reproduce – it has to be. Ultimately, the society that they evolved is going to involve sex because it is so vital to living beings.

Once you toss a bunch of beings together, the hormones (or equivalent) get going and there's mating behavior, competition, childrearing, and more. Society, that giant organizational tool of living beings, is going to have to cope with sex and make sure it's handled properly (well, what people deem properly). Sex got us to society, and society usually has something to say about it.

Society includes rules, guides, technology, and principles that all relate to sex. It has to because that drive is real, the urge is real, and it's already omnipresent. Society, that giant conglomeration of beings, deals with sex because it's part of its members.

Not all the social aspects of sex, the taboos and erotica and the like will make sense. Some may be quite dumb. But they will be there.

When you design living creatures and their society, sex is going to come into it all the time. You can't avoid it because sex is how you got here. We'll go into detail on that in the next section, but here are some things to think about.

Exercise: List three major sexual taboos in your culture you can think of. Why do they exist?

Exercise: What is the most nonsensical sexual taboo you've seen? Why did it exist, and who may think it made or makes sense?

Conclusion

Once you have living creatures that reproduce, you eventually get society. It seems that's kind of inevitable because sex requires socialization, and society just kind of follows.

Ultimately this loops itself and the society has to handle sexual issues as well. It's sort of a perfect ouroboros really.

Now, let's talk about sex and society in detail.

Sex, Society, And Areas Of Interest

In the last section I discussed the complex elements of sex and society. Sex is a kind of primal element of living creatures, and thus affects how they develop, interact, and work together. Sentient creatures, so my thesis goes, are basically about communication, and sex is just the first form of it. Because it is so core to living beings, sex infuses a lot of what sentient beings do – and the complex structures that evolve and develop as they make societies and civilizations.

When it comes to worldbuilding cultures and society, reproduction and sex will inevitably be a part of what you create, because you don't have members of a society without making more members of society, along with all the complications that ensues. Sex may be simple in principle, but it gets pretty complicated once you have a whole lot of creatures coming together to have it. Or not have it. Or whatever.

So to help you, the worldbuilder, devise the sides of your society that involve sex (and tangentially that will be *a lot* to judge by humans), here is a list of areas to consider. This is not a complete list, just a way to get you to develop the traditions, language, and so on for your society.

The fact that this is not a complete list gives you an idea of what you may face.

First, though, let's ask the thorny question: when designing a civilization or a culture or a society, just how much do you need to think about all of this? When you consider all the traditions, habits, words, and so on that involve sex, it can be pretty exhausting to try and detail how a society handles sex. So how much do you need to do so you can get on to other stuff?

You can't spend all your time thinking about sex, even when you feel you could if it was about you having it. You've got magic and solar systems and the like to design.

In this case, I advise a few things:

1) Understand the basic attitude the society has about essential sexual issues.
2) Detail the elements relevant to "manifest" that attitude clearly.
3) Know "just a bit more" than you think your reader will need to know so you have a buffer of knowledge to help ensure you don't have gaps.

Number one is really important because, if you need to figure something out, you're primed to figure out the answers for things you didn't think of.

And with that said, let's get going . . .

Society And Sex Checklist
Here are areas that you'll need to consider when designing sex and societies in your world. It's not complete, but it should be enough to keep you going.

Of course this is derived from our own human experience. Mileage may vary when you get to the Wizard-cephalopods of the Nebula of Storms.

Lineage
Most forms of reproduction we may conceive involve close lineages – someone is the offspring of so-and-so, who is the off-spring of such-and-such, going back in time. Sex means someone gets out there and produces the generation that produces the next one. Chances are lineage is tied to a lot of important things.

Consider the battles over kingships and inheritances you've seen or read about in our world. Think about the obligations people have in your culture towards family members. Lineage is often part of the human experience; what about the world you're creating?

Is lineage important in your setting? If not, no worry; but if it is important (or instinctual), then how does it affect society, traditions, laws, and so on?

Exercise: Ask how many times you've dealt with lineage-based issues in your life, such as wills, inheritance, paternity, and so on.

Birth

At some point a new life comes into being. So what does the society do then? Considering how much reproducing a society may do, there's going to be a lot to do and thus are born traditions, rules, and more.

Birth means you suddenly have a new member of society, and if you're anything like humans, one that's rather vulnerable and needs to be raised and spits up on stuff. It also brings in the complications of lineage, medical issues, and more. Birth is so complicated people may forget what the person giving birth is going through.

It's very likely a society is going to construct a lot of traditions and policies around birth. Birth is the end result of sex and the beginning of a lot of other questions.

Exercise: Last time you or a close friend or relative had a child, what social, religious, and cultural activities did you engage in? What purpose did they serve (if any)?

Raising Offspring

Once you've got new members of society, your various species and beings and societies are going to raise them. Perhaps there is, again, some difference between the people you write and humanity, but if not, then you're back to the issue of raising kids. If they need raising.

Raising children is about taking new members of society, ensuring the function within it, and make it to adulthood functional.

Child-rearing influences and is influenced by other elements of society. It's the morals to be passed on, the education to be formalized, the principles learned. Raising children is the end result of sex – and how societies reproduce as well.

It's not just genes. In some ways, genes are the carriers of society.

Exercise: How did you get raised to be who you are? What worked and what didn't? Why did the traditions and things you experienced exist (even if it wasn't a good reason)?

Puberty (Or The Lack Thereof)

Puberty among humans is something we take for granted because we're used to it. Every joke or lamentation about it seems so standard that we miss what it is: a child beginning the transformation into an adult capable of reproduction and participating in society.

That's actually pretty impressive, but we tend not to think about it, though maybe we're just trying not to remember how dumb we acted when the hormones hit us.

It's likely any species you design has some kind of change into having full maturity and reproductive capacity. If this isn't part of a species you design, then that alone brings in a lot of complexities. Have a sentient species that can reproduce right after birth and you have some seriously complicated issues. At that point you've got human Tribbles.

(Feel free to use that idea.)

I'm going to focus on puberty or the equivalent in your settings, assuming a setting you created has creatures that take time to reach physical, mental, and sexual maturity.

What is puberty? It means the transformation of a creature into a more mature form, which includes reproductive capacity. Society must cope with that because that's a big change. It's almost like the person is evolving into something else just within their lifetime.

Unless maturity comes in a proper order or all at once, sexual, mental, and physical maturity may arrive at different times. As we can see in humans, they don't always line up. We're ready to reproduce yet not at our most mentally mature. The timing of puberty, among other biological processes, is another complication to the rules society must develop.

Just look at battles over sex education in the history of many countries if you want an idea of how puberty complicates things. Well, complicates it for people not going through it.

Exercise: Think of the different rituals you've seen for puberty, the different initiations (formal and otherwise), and social concern for adolescents. Now think of what that means for a society you develop.

Adulthood
If you've got some kind of maturing process (puberty), at some point a creature in a society becomes an adult – a functional member of society (and often one able to reproduce).

172 | Steven Savage

Adulthood brings up a huge amounts of issues a society must cope with. When does someone become mature? What is needed for them to be a functional adult? How is this adulthood communicated to people? What rules about sex change at maturity?

Adulthood is when you get handed the keys to society, as it were; most societies (consciously or unconsciously, in an organized or disorganized manner) need to have systems and institutions to pull that off. Plenty of interests, and competing interests, come into play.

Adulthood, to bring it back to our subject, is often when the ability to sexually reproduce is recognized and perhaps even emphasized. The child is now a member of society. Society needless to say needs to recognize and prepare them for this – and maybe prepare itself.

Exercise: When did you find you were considered an adult, or what do you think your society requires you to do to be considered an adult?

Sexual Variance
Sex is a primal form of communication, and as we all know communication takes many forms.

Humans are sexual creatures, and sex infuses so much of what we do.

Humans in turn are sexually variable, as are many species. People can be gay, straight, biseuxal, asexual, transgendered. Humans may even change inclinations or try things out, evolving as they go, finding out more about themselves. This book was written in a time where America's perception of LGBT+ individuals was radically changing.

Society, which has an interest in maintaining itself, will in turn deal with sexual variance differently. What is accepted, what is not, what is known and what is not known – all these will affect the rules of that society. A society may embrace variance or try to stamp it out.

Either way, it will have rules and ways of dealing with it.

Exercise: How have sexual attitudes towards sexual variance in your society changed in your lifetime? How have others? Why did they exist?

Courtship
Reproduction leads to offspring, offspring grow and mature and then have more offspring. So when designing your society, you're going to have to figure out how society deals with your species finding mates, having sex, and possibly reproducing.

Societies have an interest in courtship because it usually leads to social bonding in the form of marriage or other relationships, and, in some cases, children. Actually, it can also lead to children without those social engagements, which means that society at large is kind of concerned with that as well.

It doesn't take much reading of human history to see just how much drama, conflicts, and time is dedicated to courtship. That should tell you that when you're designing a society, you have to gear up and cover courtship in potentially painful detail.

Exercise: Walk through advice sections of a bookstore and see how many are on anything related to courtship, from dating to weddings. Any species you build could have that level of detail.

Reproductive Relationships

Reproduction leads to children who grow, mature, court, and then bond/pair-bond/get married/what have you. Sentient beings enter into some kind of reproductive relationship, so for the sake of your worldbuilding I'm just going to call it marriage. It's the best word I can choose.

Societies obviously have an interest in marriage since that involves social bonding, reproduction, and the roles of people. The individuals in societies also have an interest as well because they're part of society. So you'll have to figure out how your society deals with marriage.

Marriage traditions around the world vary, and they vary in history, but their sheer prominence tells you that humans think a lot about it. These traditions may vary, but they exist everywhere. You can assume most sentient species will be likewise engaged.

When it comes to marriages, it's also important to be aware that expectations and traditions and elements of societies may not be verbalized or obvious. They can be so integral and so common that no one even knows they're there. Marriage, when you get to it, gets into everyday life; people may not even pay attention to it as it is as common as air.

Also, marriages have boundaries which you're not supposed to transgress. There are things you don't do, which often involve sex in our human societies. These things can change, such as with issues of premarital sex. Either way, there will almost certainly be boundaries.

Exercise: How many people do you know define themselves or are significantly defined by their marital relationships? How many people are defined by those relationships (such as children)?

Conception

Children who grow up, become adults, court, get married, and the system starts all over again. New life gets created. This is sort of where all of societies' attitudes about sex come together: the rules, issues, and traditions of creating new life.

Or not creating new life, as birth control, non-reproductive sex, and so on also come into the picture. As noted, sex is likely to evolve and be repurposed within the lives of sentient beings, so there are also points where you don't want conception. Just logging onto the internet will give you access to plenty of non-reproductive sex examples that you should definitely not be looking at at work.

Thus your society is going to have plenty of rules for conception, not conceiving, pregnancy, and the like. After all, that relates to members of society and how you get them (or don't get them).

Exercise: How have attitudes towards sex and conception changed in your lifetime? The lifetime of your parents? Of your country's history? Why?

Decrease/End Of Reproductive Ability

Finally, there's a point where life forms stop reproducing. Now in some cases that's death (unless we drag in cloning), but in the case of humans we often lose reproductive capacity before that point. Because this involves various biological changes, it can be pretty prominent in other ways.

Consider humans. Menopause involves the ceasing of reproductive ability and hormonal changes. Look at the concern about impotence men may have. Just consider issues of royal and family lineages affected by age.

Social rules and rituals may recognize, have penalties, or compensate for these changes. After all, they will be rather noticeable as people are having it happen to them.

This is an area where worldbuilders don't give enough thought, in my opinion. So I'm encouraging you to.

Society also will have rules about reproductive changes and transformations. What will they be?

Exercise: Where have you seen people deal with a loss of reproductive capacity, how did they react, and what social rules were involved?

Onward And Forward

This is just a limited list of major social areas where a society is going to have rules that, directly or indirectly, relate to sex. It should give you enough to think of.

I can say that sex is an area that is usually not addressed in proper detail in worldbuilding. It's too easy to map what is known or put "a twist" on an idea, or to just resort to tropes, without really exploring. A look at the fascinating history of traditions related to sex, courtship, and art shows there's a lot to build and create in your worlds.

Done right it makes richer, more believable worlds and characters. It's up to you to do the work so fictional people get to have believable sex.

Not quite fair, but you chose to be a worldbuilder.

Gods, Spirits, Sex, Magic

So we've covered biology, psychology, and society, and how they tie to sex. My fundamental thesis is that sex is best viewed as a primal form of communication for life, and thus logically infuses all aspects of said life, even to social development. Life is about transmission of information.

But there's one more element of sex and your setting to consider beyond these: the supernatural. If your world has a supernatural (or perhaps "metanatural") component, then sex is going to impact that too. Sex is part of living beings, living beings deal with metaphysical realities, and so it's going to be something you have deal with as a worldbuilder.

Got spirits? Sex is going to come into the equation as your sentient species interact with such things. Possibly to ask them for help, possibly to date them.

Got sorcery? Then is it affected by sex, sex drive, sexual energy – or are people just using magic to get dates?

This goes into so many potential areas I'm just going to cover the basics, since your worldbuilding will doubtlessly have its own elements that are unique to your work. I'm just trying to get things going here.

But first . . .

The Gods Must Be Voyeurs

One of the issues I find in writing about sex and metaphysics is people assume that the gods, angels, and demons actually give a damn about who's doing what in the bedroom. Sure, it's vital as it is part of living beings, but there's an assumption that it's a massive, vital issue to the supernatural creatures of any setting.

The gods and spirits apparently care about sex they might not be doing.

I think this attitude exists because:

- Humans figure everyone is as worked up about sex as they are, so the gods and demons must be to.
- The fact sex is a powerful drive. It infuses what we do anyway and we figure the spirits and angels care about the effect it has on us.
- Nosy people assume their religion means they can ask what you do in the bedroom and that it matters to them. They figure the gods are as nosy as they are.
- We're a bit voyeuristic and figure supernatural entities are too.

Once you get outside of the human sphere to the realm of magic and gods, be sure to take an appropriate step back and ask just how much the sex activities of your sentient species matter in those areas. It may not matter that much; in short, you may not have much worldbuilding to do about sex on the supernatural level.

We're just used to our own drives and lots of busybodies sending up cultural chaff as it were.

So with that being said, here are areas sex and metaphysics may come together in your world. If that's relevant. Otherwise, the gods and demons can go do something more interesting to them.

Subtle Forces
If you've got a world of magic and magical energies that interact with and are acted on through your sentient species, then sex may matter. Sentients use magic (or whatever), sentients have sex, ergo the two are going to come together as it were. Perhaps in horrible ways.

This could be something as simple as "do not try magic while having sexual thoughts, man, you'll be sorry" to mystic energies being part of sex itself (which can be see in real-life esoteric practices). Where there's sex and sorcery, there's a chance the two will come together, if only in warnings of why the two shouldn't come together less you have premature evocation or accidentally invoke in public.

Here's a handy checklist to keep in mind when dealing with sex and supernatural forces in designing your setting.

1) Do the mystic forces of your world interact with, affect, are affected by, or indeed power sexual activity? Why or why not?
2) What effects does sexual activity, ideas, and thoughts have on said mystical forces and what are the repercussions?
3) What social, divine, and other rules exist due to #1 and #2?
4) What social, divine, and other rules exist due to #1 and #2 but make no sense, don't do their job, or are no longer relevant?

Otherworldly Interactions

Another issue that can happen in dealing with magic and sexuality is that the otherworldly beings may also have an interest in having sex with humans. This has been a big part of human culture, from seductive succubi to the promiscuous Zeus. Sometimes, at least in human legend, the interactions of sex and the supernatural get personal on a very intimate level.

When exploring this in your setting you'll want to ask why this happens, if this happens at all. (Again, the gods may not care.) You may have some vague ideas, but ask these questions:

1) Why do these otherworldly beings want to have sex with the worldly sentients? To what point? What is the reason?
2) Why are they physically compatible (or how do they become so)?

3) What happens with conception? Dealing with half-human pregnancy can be a Herculean effort, massively lame pun intended.

In many cases, the supernatural creatures you're writing might be considered another sentient species; perhaps, like we humans and your sentients, sex is a big part of their lives and drives. Just with more dimensional gates.

The Cycle Of Life

Sex leads to pregnancy, which leads to new life, and this can be pretty important in a supernatural setting. New life means a new mind, new body, and a new member of society. This impacts the supernatural as well since the supernatural is part of your setting.

If yours is a world of reincarnation, pregnancy isn't jut a birth, it's a return. "OK, let's see who it is this time . . ."

If supernatural creatures prey around the edges of the human mind, a new mind can be vulnerable, or perhaps the best defense. "The demons are coming, get me a troop of happy babies to form a barrier!"

If everyone in your setting has magical power, including children, pregnancy and birth get a lot more dangerous. Could a child cast spells in the womb? If so, that makes reincarnation even more problematic. "Oh, poor thing, her child was a wizard in a former life and now she's got intermittent thaumaturgy."

Sex and pregnancy are probably complicated enough in your setting, and throwing in sorcery and demons and ghosts makes it far more complicated.

Here are some questions to help you out:

1) How do the metaphysics and magics of your world affect conception, pregnancy, and birth?
2) How do young minds affect or are affected by the supernatural realities of your setting?
3) How has society coped with #1 and #2? For that matter, has it coped at all?

God Games

If the gods or equivalent beings of your setting made the setting then they made the sentients – and made sex, which is how you get sentients.

So, why did they do this anyway? Why did they make sex the way they did (well, the way you did, but you know what I mean)?

If your setting involves a creationist scenario, why do the gods and demons and beings that made humanity care about sex? Why does it work the way it does? What does that mean for morals and ethics? What does that mean for society?

There are many options, so it's going to be an individual-case scenario. But if the gods made the sex drive of your sentients, then it all exists for a good reason. In turn, you need to know why as a worldbuilder to design and understand your setting.

There's *plenty* to design, and plenty of rich stories to explore. Maybe the sex drive of your sentients was corrupted. Or the gods didn't consult each other properly. Or it's well-designed and in your setting some issues we have with sex your sentient species don't. Who knows?

But if the gods got into the making game, you have to look at sex and ask why everything works that way deliberately and how and why the gods made things they way they are.

Figure that out and you've got a rich sense of detail that makes your world really alive.

A few questions to help you out.

1) What role did the supernatural in your world play in creating sex?
2) What interest does the supernatural have in sex?
3) What role do supernatural forces in your world play in affecting, regulating, and monitoring the sex of sentients?
4) Do all the supernatural forces have the same interests in the sexual activity of mortals?
5) What conflicts result from #1, #2, #3, and #4?

Big Picture, Big Question

Once again this all comes full circle, from dealing with sentients reproducing to asking the big questions of life. This is a normal part of worldbuilding, big and small pictures interacting.

As I hammer at repeatedly, sex is part of sentient beings, so if there are metaphysical realities in your world those will affect and be affected by sex. You'll need to address these when appropriate or there will be a huge gap in your setting and stories within it. Addressing them, on the other hand, makes for a richer world.

Just because your reader thinks one thing doesn't mean they know what's going on. That's part of the fun! We always make assumptions about sex, and shattering assumptions properly can pleasantly surprise the reader.

Species And Races

Let's Talk About Species And Races – Kind Of

And now, let's talk about building sentient races in your world. Or sentient species. Or . . . well, it gets complicated.

Building "races" is a big thing in worldbuilding, especially in the areas of Science Fiction and Fantasy. People craft epically different alien races. Games have different stats for the "player races." Everyone seems happy when some fantasy world has Not Just Another Elf, since so many races seem the same in such settings.

If you're worldbuilding, there's a chance you need to create races. That's the problem. When we talk about worldbuilding races, we're not *always* talking *races*. If I'm going to talk about how to populate our settings, we need to clarify what we're talking about.

I'm probably not talking about what you think I am. In fact, I won't be.

A Matter Of Terminology

The term race, if you want to get technical (and I do) refers to a group within a species that has certain identifiable characteristics. It's "here's an identifiable population of a species with similar traits." Race is <u>part</u> of species, and the definition of a race is highly subjective.

Let's talk about the word "race" where it most comes up in worldbuilding: constructing aliens and non-humans in science fiction and fantasy settings. We talk about the elven race, or the Klingon race or the Grashuka Race of the Gas Giants. We toss the word "race" around so much when building these settings, one issue gets missed.

We're often using the word race wrong.

Note the above definition of race; it's a way to identify populations within a species. The problem is, when we think we're building races, we're actually building *species*.

Maybe you knew this (and I hope you did), but the word "race" gets tossed around casually and I want to address this.

Those giant cephalopod philosophers from Aldebaran that you created are not race, they're a *species* (that may contain races). They don't come from the same origins as humans, and scientifically they couldn't even crossbreed with us. They are not just distinct, they are literally an *entire alien species*.

But we might call them a race. Even I, typing this, find myself slipping into using "race" when I mean species (indeed, I had to re-edit this book several times because of that). I blame the way the word's been casually tossed around, which I think is both honest, yet allows me to feel slightly less guilty.

Oh, and to make things more complicated, sometimes we **treat** species like races.

Everyone On The Xenophilia Train
There's a strong element of SF and fantasy fiction that involves the interbreeding of different species. Demons have children with humans, elves with humans, and . . . well, we humans apparently will breed with anything in media. Either way, a lot of creative works have different species interbreeding with other species.

That makes everything a bit more complicated, because though humans may be made by one god and the Elves are crystallized starlight, these species are able to reproduce as if they were *races* – separate populations of the same species. This kind of muddles the terminology up.

Sure, this may not be "realistic" from a scientific point of view, but that doesn't stop people from creating it. Science Fiction has been having human/alien crossbreeding long before Spock's dad decided to get earthbound. In media, the boundary between species and race is a bit fuzzy when it comes to reproducing.

This makes terminology a bit different. After all, when do you call something a race and call something a species? Especially when, say, you're working on a giant book on worldbuilding?

So What Do We Do Here?

I called this out because it's important and because it's a pet peeve, but what we do here is choose terms carefully. If I want to discuss creating species (or races) I have to pick the right terms, and if we want to communicate as worldbuilders, we need to use the right language.

Ultimately, for this section, I'll be using the word "species" to discuss species, and "race" to indicate distinct populations in that species. It's time to use proper terminology because it improves communication – and if you say "race" when you mean "species," then how do you even talk about race which is already quite subjective?

What You Have To Look Out For

So, as a worldbuilder, here's what you need to look out for when building species.

1) Does your setting have species or races in the classic sense- are the various creatures and sentients in your setting of common origins or different ones? That will help you design them better, and realize when there are radical differences.
2) Does your setting allow for the species/race boundary to be less than clear? If your fantasy races can all interbreed because of magic, then you'll need to keep that in mind. There may be species whose interbreeding is more like races.

188 | Steven Savage

3) What are the impacts of #1 and #2? If you have exotically different alien species who can all interbreed, what does that mean for their societies, for genetic health, and for children? For that matter, it brings in a whole new definition of "First Contact."

4) What terminology do people use to refer to their race/species depending on how distinct the identity is? Right here we just discussed race versus species; others in your world are going to have that debate.

In the end you need to know when you have species, when you have races, and when you have species that act like races.

Yes, it's confusing. But it's less confusing than not pausing to ask the race/species question.

So with this out of the way, let's get into the nitty gritty of species creation.

Species – Getting The Setting

Now, with the issue of race and species cleared up by using the right terminology, let's talk designing species. As in distinct, interbreeding creatures of a common origin. The *proper* term.

I've covered some of this elsewhere in addressing intelligent life, which I assume is largely what we're covering here. In this case, we're going to get into the details about species creation.

Species start with the setting. After all, that's where they come from.

Getting And Vetting The Setting

Species are the products of their setting. They are born of it, defined within it, interact with in it, change within it – and, perhaps, end with it. Much as I note that your world is your main character, you need to know it to understand why species are the way they are. Species don't spring to being out of the void, they come from somewhere; just as art is the expression of an artist, races are an expression of the setting.

They're the children of your setting, as it were.

Where It Begins

Species, these defined, identifiable, unique set of creatures have to come from somewhere. To have this, you have to look at your setting and ask 1) how the world works and 2) what forces bring the races into being. Where does the spark of life begin and what kind of light does it emit?

Are you writing a real world science setting? Then you'll need to do research on the evolutionary science of your setting to create realistic species, and figure how to explain it to people without sounding like a textbook. Such a work well may seem a bit like writing a science paper, but that's what you elected to do.

Are you doing a setting where the gods made everything? Then you'll need to figure how they agreed (and disagreed) on what to make and who species-wise. What were their goals and plans, intentions and mistakes, hopes and failures in making life?

Intelligent Design is a *lot* more complicated to write as you have to write the Intelligent Designers.

Are you doing soft science, where you can nod to evolution but still get a bit crazy with inbreeding aliens and the like? Then you'll need to figure how far to go science-wise versus using space opera tropes, and what this means for your species. As noted, when your supposedly different species behave like races when it comes to inbreeding, things get complicated.

(Let's face it, if inbreeding among aliens was/is easy, you know humans would take First Contact into Second Contact, Third Contact, and Make You Breakfast In The Morning Contact.)

This is important because otherwise your species aren't "part" of the setting, they're just a pile of traits with no grounding nor reason. Much as shoving characters into a setting with no connection feels "wrong," it's the same with species.

An example I like to invoke is J.R.R. Tolkien's dwarves. Created by a god of craft and metal who wanted his own children to love, they reflected his obsessions, and were a bit imperfect as a species. They had an origin in setting that, in turn, reflected traits that made sense. They seemed real in their own mono-mythical setting.

(And yes, if you think of a species as being a character in a way, you've just realized an excellent way to understand your setting – be it science or magic.)

Species are unlikely to be stagnant. They have stories and backstories, changing over time. Just like characters.

The Development Of Species

Unless your story starts off at the moment of creation, your species have history and changes that affect them. They came to be – and they are shaped by what happens to them. They become different over time, perhaps quite quickly.

Wars, good years, plagues, discoveries, ice ages, magical accidents, wars of gods and demons – all these shape a species. They can triumph or suffer, breed prodigiously or be nearly wiped out. They are changed by mutation, population decreases, variant gene pools, and more.

So once you determine your species' origin, you need to think how they were shaped over time.

- How much time passed since they came to be and your tales? A lot can happen in even a short time, so what did occur that affects them?
- What events happen in the world that can shape them? Are there constants that will always affect them, or are there major changes that will suddenly alter the rules?
- How did these events shape them?
- Are these events preserved/remembered in their culture?

This is where understanding your setting is vitally important because it shapes the species in it (and in turn, this shapes the characters of those species). A setting is a living thing in it's way, species are alive in their way, and the former shapes the latter into new forms as time passes.

In our world, you can see many ways human history shaped who we are. There was the past offshoot, the Neanderthals. We survived ice ages and climate changes and plagues. There's always some discussion of how "gene pool X" came to be based on some famous events.

Your setting will affect your species similarly, sculpting them delicately or brutally into something that may be quite different than when they started. There may not even be a "start," but a long series of changes as the species adapt.

And on the subject of adaption . . .

Fit Is It

When you're asking about how your setting spawns and changes your species, there's also the question of fit. How does the species fit into the setting – a species has to live within the setting after all.

Maybe the species was created to fit perfectly into the setting, so there's few changes that affect them (meaning any big changes might be near-unsurvivable). Of course this may not matter if the gods are running everything, but still, the gods may not be perfect.

Maybe the species was exposed to many mild, but effective evolutionary pressures in a hard-science setting, and so is extremely adaptable. Over time, the changes inflicted upon them make them good at surviving changes. A species like that could be so adaptable they might seem like a collection of different species.

Maybe the species is a vital part of the setting ecosystem, maybe as caretakers or important to predators. How does this fit affect them as they grow and change? When a species that's a prey animal evolves enough to take on the predators, interesting things may be afoot for the setting (and the predators get a nasty surprise).

Maybe they're just hanging on, battling against the odds. Perhaps they'll fade, or triumph and then promptly try and change their setting radically to survive further.

In turn, species will affect their world, if only to survive. Look at how we humans have altered our own, possibly to our own detriment.

What species do and how they it – and how they make themselves fit into a setting – is important to understanding them. Species and setting is a kind of dialogue, each changing the other, so you need to know where the species fits into the big picture.

Even if it's a poor fit.

A Quick Note: Change Is Always
Species will change in many cases. Who they were eons, centuries, or even decades ago may not be who they are now. The gene pool changes, ethnic distribution alters, and technology changes survival traits.

It may be worth keeping a timeline of how your species changed if you've got a hyper-detailed setting. It makes you think and is a good reminder, if only of "what was I thinking?"

It Starts Where It Starts – And Goes Many Places
All your species start with your setting and what it contains. They derive from it, grow within it, fit in it, and perhaps die in it. Much like a character.

However, most species that you'll create are adaptable. I'd like to address that as it's often a complicator . . .

Species – Adaptable It Is

Sentient species will *probably* by very adaptable. They are going to learn, change, grow, and evolve – not just as a species, but on their own. A species can adapt with a high rate of reproduction and a good bit of mutation, but when it's sentient, the individuals and the species are likely highly adaptable.

Look at we humans. We're pretty adaptable and we're sentient, even if we make some bad choices.

Adaption is, in part, the very definition of sentience: taking in, processing, and using information. It's hard to separate sentience and adaptability, because sentience without some kind of adaptability would make a creature more akin to a machine.

When writing your sentient species you're going to want to make sure they're adaptable (unless, of course, they are like machines, in which case you've got another set of issues). Even if the gods created them, they probably need some adaptability because otherwise the gods have to make sure they don't keep wandering off of cliffs.

(Really, if you're a god, do you want most of your divine life to be like a bad version of a computer game?)

Thinking Adaptable

So think what adaption is going to mean for your species, both in general and in specific. That will help you create more believable species.

This "sentient adaptability means:"

- The ability to be aware of environment and self, and their interaction.
- The ability to process that information in order to make decisions.
- The ability to implement new behaviors.
- The ability to retain information for reference.
- The ability to communicate with and learn from others.
- The ability to implement technical systems to reach goals and adapt better.
- The ability to modify the systems above.

Pretty simple, right? Wait, there's more. Though species may be adaptable, they're going to adapt in their own way. The setting they were born from, and the way they changed, affects just how they adapt.

We humans are visual and auditory creatures. But how would we adapt and learn if, say, we became consciously aware of the electromagnetic spectrum? If we had a better sense of smell? If we could relay information telepathically?

There may also be species traits that affect what they have to adapt to. A species with a super-powerful immune system won't develop medicine the same way. A species naturally inclined to violence may have trouble with negotiations to prevent a war even if the war will wipe them out.

Your species will adapt, but they will adapt in their own unique way. It may even be ways that seem incredibly strange and weird. So don't just assume your sentient species adapts, ask how they adapt. There may be advantages and there may be limits.

That's part of the fun.

Let's take a look at the one really adaptable sentient species we know – humans. We're a good example for worldbuilders, and the only example we have right now.

The Human Touch

Humans are a great example of an adaptable species as stated.

Our adaptability has made it so we, as a species, can change and grow so much it seems like individuals and groups can act like different species.

We exist in every environment there is, from grasslands to the cold of space. Our ability to create technology and learn makes this possible.

We can be hunters and lawyers, doctors and sculptors, martial artists and writers.

We can change who we are. The writer of today may be a cook in a few years or a programmer after a decade.

If humans run across something we can't do? We make a machine or band together and do it.

And yet we're all *human*.

Though I'm aware we humans only have one sentient species (us) as an example, I'd say we make a pretty good argument that sentient species are going to be adaptable. We've survived quite a bit, adapting and changing, to the point where the biggest threat to us is, well, us.

It's sort of a triumph.

As we've evolved, we've developed the ability to evolve <u>more</u>. We make institutions and training and education to help us grow faster. Our adaptability in turn has allowed us to create tools of adaption – cars and medical devices and computers.

So it's a good assumption any sentient species will be adaptable.

I'd also note that it probably just seems more believable. We humans only have us as an example, so we're going to assume for now that a sentient species will be a bit like us – adaptability included.

Keep Adaption In Mind

When designing sentient species, remember that they'll almost certainly be adaptable. Maybe not as we humans are, but they'll be adaptable nonetheless. That's what sentience is.

Plus we at least have <u>us</u> as an example, which is a good one.

Species, Race, And Culture

Welcome to the section with the Most Controversial Sounding Title yet. Much like my sections on sex, this is probably going to be far more pedestrian than expected. Which is the point.

What we're going to talk about here is our species, their races (the subjectively-defined populations within species), and culture.

Why?

Because race (as in variants of a species) and culture gets mixed up <u>way</u> too easy. People treat race and culture the same, especially when they embarrass us at the dinner table by talking about "those people." You don't want to make the same mistake in your worldbuilding.

Yeah, I'm gonna keep it clinical if I can. So let's take a step back before moving forward.

What Is Culture?

I've covered culture before, but the best way to think of culture here is a tool. Culture is language and rules and institutions that help a sentient species interact with each other and their environment. Sure, the culture may act to the detriment of some or many, or it may backfire, but it is basically useful up to a point.

As noted, a sentient species is almost inevitably adaptable (at least as far as we can guess), and I think a sentient species inevitably has to have the ability to create, retain, and modify culture. A culture accumulates tools and wisdom, allowing a species to function. This cultural ability is needed for sentience – because you need tools like language and such to really be sentient.

In short, the ability to have culture is part of sentience. Human ability to have and modify culture means we can be hunters or astronauts, accountants or weavers, as needed. Culture is software we've written ourselves for ourselves.

Admittedly, it's often buggy and constantly being patched, but still.

So when you write sentience, you write culture. And when you create species, you create races, as the species will differ among groups. Species will also differ in their cultures and subcultures, and those may line up with racial differences.

This is when things can get unpleasant.

Culture Within Culture, Race Within Species
Let's talk race (as in populations within a species) and culture. This may be difficult to discuss as, because of many people's experiences, it's a bit hard to discuss race.

So I'm just going to do it. Oh, and if you ask why some people have an issue discussing race, you'll learn a lot . . .

Any species you design will have distinct groups will emerge – races. These groups are not different species, but are distinctly different in appearance, location, and some traits. This is because different groups will face different pressures and needs in their environments.

An isolated population may develop distinct appearances based on a limited gene pool. A mountainous environment may provide evolutionary pressures to develop better lungs. Distinct populations will doubtlessly become more distinct in time.

These groups, in being distinct, will almost certainly have distinct cultures because of their different experience. Region, location, traits, and so on will affect said culture. The very things that led to development of race (geographic isolation, section for some traits) will also affect culture – adaptability is part of sentience.

And you have to create that unique culture that the race *may* have, if it's passed on to their members. But the culture and the race aren't the same.

Merely look at the sweep of human experience. We have many variant populations (which we often spend time arguing about which is what). We have humans creating different cultures in distinct groups. As you design races and their cultures you need to know where *race and culture begin and end*.

Why? Because a lot of people are really bad at this. That family member or friend that makes insensitive racial remarks, who conflates culture with race because "those people are like this" and so on? Some worldbuilders can be as bad to their fictional creations, and that gives them a chance to annoy and confuse far more people than one insensitive relative.

Race is not culture and both are highly subjective.

Similar pressures affect them, but they are not the same. For any adaptable species, it's likely that cultures may be distinct (because of said adaptability), but the races may not be as different as one may think because of that core ability to adapt.

Your species will have many races. The variance that produces races also acts to vary cultures. The variance of race and variance of culture may at times align, but they're not the same. Much as humans who leave the environment they're born in may turn out radically different than if they had stayed, members of a race with distinct culture will be quite different if they leave.

202 | Steven Savage

If you're not careful, your creation of species, races, and cultures can quickly become a pile of stereotypes. Race and culture become the same thing, and next thing you know your races are so distinct and different they might as well be different species.

Worse, you might not realize you straightjacketed yourself until it's too late.

The mark of a mature worldbuilder is to be able to scale between environment and characters and culture, and understand where they come together without turning them into a lockstep machine. It's not easy, but it's well worth it.

You'll also avoid those horrible moments of realizing your work is as racist/hidebound/limited as those people who make you cringe.

How Does Your Species Handle Race?

You, in your wisdom as all-powerful worldbuilder, may understand the different between races and species. However, how does your species handle it?

The question you also have to ask when building a species is how its cultures and members handle the diverse races that they have. How does the species as a species and the cultures within it cope with its own diversity?

Maybe the species has strong instincts that help it work together, or it has a sense of tribalism that means at times it comes to blows.

Maybe the species' diversity is so huge that it's hard for it to shatter into identifiable racial groups. Or maybe it's settled into distinct gene pools that verge on speciation.

Or maybe it's telepathic so it's hard for it to fragment at all (and if it did, well, look out as hive minds battle).

This is a question for both your species biologically and the culture(s) that its members have. Now this is going to lead to extremely unpleasant things to consider. A quick view of human history shows many times that one group was more than willing to haul off and kill another. Our ability to recognize "like me" seems a bit close to home in a way that can threaten our own survival as big "tribes" face off.

But these issues are ones you have to deal with: how the races in your world and their culture handle the very fact they exist.

Unpleasantness aside, deciding on how these issues are handled makes a rich world and a whole ream of stories. One good misunderstanding, one tribal conflict, one species unified and reaching for the stars can come to life and make your world awesome.

Well, awesome in detail. It might suck for the species in there. Go figure.

It's Worth Doing Right

When you do race and culture well, it can be amazing. Your world becomes richer, more interesting, and your species, its races, and cultures more believable and alive.

I think it's the differences that make your species become believable. We know the diversity of our world, and seeing the diversity of another is even more enthralling and relatable.

However, we're often too willing to accept simple racial and cultural ideas. Here's another Set Of Elves. Another Not Quite The Vulcans. You can probably get by in worldbuilding with basic work.

But if you want to go farther, dive on in.

The Trap Of Positive Stereotypes

Last section I talked about how people could mix up races and culture in their worldbuilding, creating, essentially, racial stereotypes. My advice was:

- Don't do it.
- Be sure not to mix up culture versus racial/species traits.
- Really, don't do it.
- Did I mention conflating culture and biological traits is really bad?
- Don't do it.

However, there's a specific kind of stereotyping of races and/or cultures I want to call out in worldbuilding. One that's insidious in real life and in fictional world creation. One that often goes unexplored.

Stereotypes that are *positive*.

The Positive Stereotype

Some years ago I was reading a discussion about Pasta Commercials. Yes, this is relevant, hang in there.

The discussion was about stereotypes in Pasta Commercials, which were inevitably about Italian-American. The families were big and boisterous. There was a mother who cooked. There was probably one guy named Tony. Tony and company were friendly. There was a lot of good food.

The person had seen a giant pile of stereotypes. Tropes given form hawking overpriced spiced tomato sauce. Something just as stereotypical as any racist social media conversation you'd block from that one annoying relative.

206 | Steven Savage

Except the stereotypes were often positive. Togetherness. Family. Friendly people. Good food. Yes, there were a lot of tropes, but they were *positive*. Not the negative stereotypes we're all used to dealing with.

Tony and his family seemed to be pretty great people but it was all stereotypes.

This stuck with me as you see it in fictional peoples and cultures. It can be that elves are always crack archers, or this alien species is highly intelligent or what have you. There are many races, species, and cultures in fiction that are stereotypical or have become stereotypical, but many of these stereotypes are positive.

And I think they're lousy thing to do as a worldbuilder.

Let's talk how positive stereotypes screw you up.

The Power Of Positive Stereotypes (Is Awful)

We're all familiar with Negative Racial And Cultural Stereotypes in worldbuilding. By the tenth greedy dwarf, or the latest Big Headed Super Smart Alien With No Emotions, we're sick of stereotypes. It's practically a joke among genre fans.

But positive stereotypes? Well, those bear more exploration. Here's where they can cause problems in your worldbuilding.

A Stereotype Is A Stereotype: Positive, negative, what have you, when your races/species/cultures are stereotypes it is a *limit on you and your setting*. They become less a living thing and more a list of tropes. They are no longer not part of their world, but just some disconnected ideas you ram into your setting. They derail your world and make it less alive.

Positive Invisibility: We're used to looking for negative stereotypes as we see their bad (both as writers and from real life). Positive stereotypes are ones we can miss as we're looking for the bad or we assume they're complimentary. They're not always complimentary. Ask anyone who's been told "I bet *you* people are really good at . . ."

Warning Sign: A positive stereotype may mean you or your readers apply other stereotypes to the characters in your world. Strong means dumb. Agile means you're a tree-hugger who carries bows. Applying positive stereotypes may mean you as a worldbuilder bring in related baggage. Worse, your readers will, and they wonder why you had one stereotype but not another. This might not be conscious, but still.

Bad Form: Either way, relying on stereotypes makes you lazy. Don't do it. It limits you.

Embarrassment: Finally, when you rely on any stereotypes you run the risk of embarrassment. People will see the flaws in your logic, the mistakes, the issues, and the relying on stereotypes. Even positive stereotypes are still something that says "this person is unimaginative."

It's OK, It Happens, But . . .

Work to avoid positive stereotypes as well as negative ones. They have their own effects – some quite insidious. When it comes down to it, worldbuilding with stereotypes, again, is *bad*.

Will you do it? Of course you will. You can just be aware of it and keep getting better.

Characters

Where The Characters Are – And What?

You have built a world. You know its origins and its ecology, you know its peoples and their religion, and you know the technology or sorcery (or both) that they use. You have a setting that is a living, breathing creation, in your head, and your documents, and your stories.

It's time to populate it with characters. You've probably started early, but there's always time to think about how to make them better. Or you may need to restart now that you've built the world so much as some of your earlier ideas just don't fit.

Most of us creating worlds have them populated with people to tell stories about or to play (in the case of the game). Characters are often both the start and the result of worldbuilding. To do them right, we should examine their role in the world, in the stories and games we derive from the world, and what they mean to the audience.

What Is A Character?

So, what is a character in all of this anyway?

I've said earlier that characters are lenses on your setting, and your setting in a way is the main character. Characters provide views and interact with the setting. They're the people that your audience relates to and sees the world through. They are *expressions* of the world you've made.

You may seem them for only a moment, hear only a few words, but every decent character is a "someone."

212 | Steven Savage

Having someone people relate and connect to is vital for good storytelling, and few authors can pull off a story without someone in it people can connect to. If you're creating games, it's even more important since this is essentially your connection to the world you're influencing.

Breaking it down, a character is:

• Someone for the reader/player/media participant to relate to, understand the world through, and even interact with or through.
• A viewpoint on the world. A character may not "get" the entire setting, but that's the point. Indeed, this unique viewpoint makes them more relatable.
• The result of their world. Characters are quite literally a product of their environment; they act as a summary of the world in some ways. This means they are viewpoints, but knowing them automatically reflects the setting.

Characters are the part of the world that you "get" the world through.

Each of these is important as a world creator as:

• If a character can't be related to or provide a viewpoint, the viewer can't get the story or the world you've created. If you've read a tale where a character seems abstractly stuck into an unrelated environment, then you know what I mean.
• If a character doesn't have a viewpoint that is "theirs," then the experience of the world and their life is disjointed. Think about all those stories or games where a character just knew something they shouldn't and it just felt wrong.
• If a character doesn't seem to be a part of their world, then you know how that grates. The tale becomes almost unreliable and hard to understand. Though this can be used for humor, it can be done wrong . . . and usually is.

Characters will have radically different levels of detail. Some random policeman or bartender may be a name and some traits, while your protagonist has a rich history. But both need to have reasons and viewpoints, even if one is "really hates owning this bar and that's all I know."

Characters are both the results of the world and the portals to it. But a character doesn't just stand there. Characters are alive in your world. That's where your worldbuilding comes to full fruition . . .

Characters Interact With The World

A character really is the result of all the processes and principles, science and sorcery, gods and science, coming together to result in some intelligent being that you can tell tales about. They are the result of the world, a lens on it, and they affect and change it.

That's where your worldbuilding comes full circle. You have built this giant setting, characters come from it, and in turn the characters change it. In fact, in a game that's often the point.

If you have built your world well, it not only provides a setting for your characters to come from and helps them "be," but it also reacts to them. If someone violates a law in your carefully crafted culture, you know the reaction. If someone wields mighty magics to change weather, you know it will affect an oncoming army of very unhappy dragons. If someone discovers a horrible truth, you know how their mind may warp, and what they may do (possibly involving an army of rain-hating dragons, just noting).

Now that you have these lenses, these viewpoints, these tight little spheres of "continuity" called characters, things happen as they interact with each other and the setting. Because you know this world well, you can write the interactions.

These interactions and effects? *They're the stories you tell or play out.*

If you've done intense worldbuilding, you know that in many cases this is an incredible experience. The stories nearly write themselves. Events unfold. You know what interactions to put into the game. Everything comes full circle and it just lives; you merely record it.

This is why good character development is the summary of good worldbuilding. They are where the world comes to life, in an understandable way, and their interactions with the world tell the tales you craft and the plots people play.

If you can master world creation, character creation, and writing, then your tales can take on a life of their own.

But in the midst of the rush, some caution . . .

Character Creation – Warnings

When you create your characters, there are a few things that can go wrong. I'll cover character creation tips next section, but the warnings are important.

Here are things that can sabotage you:

Character First: Oftentimes we have character ideas without a well fleshed out setting. This happens, but you can end up making the idea of the character more important than their setting. Avoid this temptation and embrace the world you created; an ill-fitting character disrupts your world and your writing, and the disjointed experience can be jarring. Be willing to embrace the character's evolution as their world takes shape, revising them and ensuring they're part of it.

The Unsouled: A flipside is to look at your setting and sort of conjure up some characters to fit it and flesh out your roster. Characters should be people as well, not cardboard cutouts with a few bits of continuity tacked on. I find the best way to avoid this problem is to run with each character and get to know them, even if it's only a few things. If you figure some random annoying merchant is annoying because the day's late and the religious festival has taken up a lot of his time, then you're good.

The Trope Onslaught: A sort of middle ground between the last two problems, sometimes characters can be broad archetypes that are kind of alive, but kind of inserted, and not exactly "really living." There's something there since they are archetypes, but it's not quite right about them. This is an easy trap to fall into, and I usually find the best bet is to start fleshing them out and see how they grow. Sometimes this is extra fun as you can make a trope surprising.

The God Character: A constant problem is the character around whom the setting bends (and one I complain about repeatedly). To create a character with certain goals or assumptions and then bend the world around them is ultimately undermining your work, unless that is part of the larger way the world works. You can fool yourself too easily into thinking said character has a reason to be, but when you notice how they are more important than your setting, you'll come to the sad realization you're writing a god wearing a mortal costume. A god character can render the setting meaningless.

The Gap: When you design characters, flesh them out using your world knowledge. Leaving too many gaps, or leaving them as broad assumptions, can show up and often derail your writing, coding, and future worldbuilding. I find much as it is with worlds, take character design a bit farther to do more than the reader needs to see so you, as a writer, know enough.

There's many other challenges you can face. These are just the ones I've noticed and experienced as the most common.

Closing

A character brings the world full circle, creating a part of the setting that is alive, that people experience the story through, and that you can in turn have change the world by interacting with it. Indeed, people interacting with each other and the world is a story.

There are ways to get derailed, but being aware of them can help you avoid the problems.

Of course, building characters takes effort. In fact, everyone seems to have their own way to do it. Next section, I'll talk about some techniques that may help.

Character Creation

After spending last section talking about characters in worldbuilding, it's time to talk about creating characters in detail in your world.

Of all the worldbuilding tasks, character creation is the one that can (and in my opinion, should) be the most complex. As noted, a character is in a way the summary of the setting, and in turn, extremely complicated. They're little balls of condensed continuity rocketing around your world.

Characters are your setting come to visible, relatable life. Each is a personal, little world.

The problem in discussing how to create characters is that the process itself is also unique for everyone. I can't give you a system that will do it for you. In fact, I shouldn't because we all do this differently.

What I can do is give a list of techniques I've used, encountered, and coached on to help you create good characters. Some you're doing. Some you aren't. Some will work. Some won't, but would work for someone else.

But you can find what works for you.

I said this wasn't simple. People never are, and that's what you're creating.

Character Creation: A Long List Of Techniques

So let's get to what can help you with conjuring forth a cast.

The List

Some people have ideas for characters they jot down and use later. Sure the characters are a quick summary, but they are something to use later. Try keeping a list of character ideas, reviewing it regularly, and tapping it as needing.

Also remember that characters and settings interact. Adding a character from your list may alter your setting, hopefully in delightful ways.

Cautions: The characters should be "rebuilt" in your continuity to avoid the flaws of just shoving them in to whatever world you're building. Sometimes an idea is so far along they don't fit and you have to start over.

The Intersect

When you build a world, there's many times you ask "hey who did this?" Why invented Faster-Than-Light travel? Who runs this fantasy tavern with a disturbing level of fights? Who was this character's lost parent? When you are making a world, there are many blank spots that should be filled with people. Filling them in fleshes out the world and fleshes out your cast, and you have a bit of a start as you kind of know who they are in general (even if it's "weird inventor" or "put-upon bar owner").

Working with The Intersect method is not only a good way to flesh out characters, even if it's more background characters, but to understand setting/character relations.

Cautions: Avoid creating characters that are basically there to wear a hat that designates their profession. That may be fine for a background character, but in the case of anyone critical or potentially critical, make sure they become real characters.

The Spirit

Almost inevitably when we start writing we already have character ideas. It's a bit like The List method above, but more specific to the setting. Often characters and setting evolve alongside each other as one makes you think of the others and more details emerge as questions are asked. Keep a list of characters you've created and review it regularly to see where they may need to be fleshed out, remade, or detailed more.

Cautions: You can create a character a bit too much and then have them drive the setting, which was warned about earlier. Be sure to revisit and revise them as needed until they're properly "real."

The Character Sheet

A personal favorite of mine. Keep a sheet of essential character traits, a bit like a profile or a Role-Playing Game Character Sheet, and fill it out for characters you create. You may even modify the sheet for different settings. It makes you think, makes you ask questions, and gives you a nice record of character information to refer back to. Re-reading them can be very stimulating, and I find that when I can fill out a detailed character sheet for a character I usually "get" them.

If you do have to modify the sheet for different settings, that's actually helpful as a writer. It makes you ask about the world and what you need to know, which just helps you know the world better.

Cautions: If a character doesn't come to life before – or after – doing a sheet, then you don't "get" them. Keep modifying the sheets over time to incorporate new, inspiring/informative categories that help you write. These shouldn't be static.

The Questions

Very similar to the Character Sheet method, asking questions about characters until they spring to life is a popular technique, and one that is useful just for fleshing them out. What is their hobby? What is their favorite food? Over time, you can develop a list of questions for the characters you create to help you out. There are plenty of these lists out there on the internet as well.

Individual settings may, in turn, have individual questions. Fleshing these out, just like the Character Sheet method, helps you know the world better.

Keep a list of good character questions to ask if this method works for you.

Cautions: Good questions shock and surprise you. Some may become habit, and others may just be ones you fill in to get out of the way. Shake up or randomize your character questions to keep it fresh.

The Talk

Imagine you're having a conversation with one of your characters. You may even want to write it down. Try that technique, in the form of a dialogue, to see what you learn about them. It can also help you develop the proper "voice" for that character.

This method works when you have a good sense of character and the setting. If you don't, it might not be as productive, or it may help them develop. It doesn't work the same for everyone.

Cautions: Not everyone is up for this method or can use it. It can feel a bit weird to do this, after all.

The Multimedia

Try to get to know a character better by imagining them in another media form. Draw them. What actor would you cast to play them? Who would voice them? If they're a comic book character, what literary style would fit them? Try remapping the character in other media to see if it triggers any ideas.

Cautions: This method can be useful, but can also be distracting, and it risks you limiting the character based around the media you use. You can end up visualizing a character just like the actor that should play them, or get stuck on visual queues and not character ones.

The System

Similar to the Multimedia, but imagine what your character would be in a game system such as a role-playing game or other class/character-based game. This makes you think of how they're interpreted, makes you ask questions, and helps you think about them with a defined ruleset. I even met one person whose way to design characters was to ask what Pokemon™ they'd be.

(This also makes you think deeply about how game systems work and can be revealing if you're a gamer.)

Cautions: I find this is best as a stimulating exercise–. If you take it too far, your character ideas may be constrained by the very game system you're using, and some of those are very limiting.

The Jam

If you have a friend or co-author you trust, sit down and discuss characters with them to see what you come up with. A good jam with someone means you play off of each other.

Playful, creative time like this can help everyone out and provide different viewpoints.

Cautions: Different viewpoints may clash, especially if only one of you knows the world.

The Read Through
I read through my character documents now and then and just see what hits me or what I missed. I usually find some new inspiration.

Cautions: Don't do this too often or you'll sort of get numb and read what's in your head.

So there you have it, a list of techniques I use and have heard of. I'm sure there are plenty more. But I'd be remiss without adding a bit of advice on one you should use.

The Importance Of The Character Sheet
One thing I mention above is using a character sheet as a way to get to know a character. Whether that fires your imagination or not, I do recommend having some format for storing character information for your world. It's not just a brainstorming tool; it's a record-keeping tool.

Having a standard format doesn't just inspire you, it's also a list of basic things you'll need to know for writing, to have a cover artist look at, and possibly to bundle up in some world guide you release in the future. It's a record that keeps you focused and aware of what you've already created, with plenty of uses.

There's a chance it may not inspire you – that's the way it works – but finding a sheet that helps you keep track of data is important even if it's just administrative work.

Closing
There's no best way to make a character in your world. But you can find what techniques work for you and make them work.

You might even invent some new ones. If you do, be sure to share them.

A Deeper Examination Of Main Characters

As a worldbuilder, your world is a vast, interlinked creation that stands there whirling in your head or your notes. Though some people may want to hear the story of your world, most want to hear the story of people in it. There's a chance your world came about out of a desire to tell a character's story.

Either way, at some point, you have to tell a tale about what's going on. A tale requires someone to tell the tale about. In short, no matter your goals in making the world, you have to settle down and tell the stories in it.

This means a main character or characters need to be selected. It may seem strange to discuss this since so many of us have our main characters in mind when we start worldbuilding, but it's not as simple as it may seem. Let's dive a bit deeper into main characters and what they mean for worldbuilders and telling tales within our worlds.

Your main character or characters may not be who you thought.

What Is A Main Character?

As I've stated earlier, characters are like lenses on a world. It is through them that people experience your setting, including the characters themselves. The viewpoints of these characters are gateways to understanding what's going on and experiencing it.

Main characters are the lenses the actual stories you're telling are seen through.

I find this perspective very helpful because:

- It makes you immediately think of a focus for your storytelling.

226 | Steven Savage

- It gives you someone you and your audience can relate to and helps develop empathy and connection. This is necessary to experience the story and the world.
- It helps you do even more worldbuilding by climbing inside someone's head and seeing how things look. You don't just walk a mile in someone's shoes, you walk that mile in their mind.
- It helps you admit you can't write or tell everything. You choose to limit yourself to the right character or characters.

Now who is your main character? Well, that may be more challenging than you think.

Here's some issues you may face.

Is It The Chosen Ones?

The truth of a lot of writing is that many games, tales, and so on are created with a given main character or characters in mind. People already have their characters chosen, and the world is created to let their stories come to life. The worldbuilding may go far beyond them and make their stories only one of many to be told (which I think should be the case), but it often starts with the idea of a *person*.

You may think you know your main characters since you started with them, but this isn't always the case. As you build your setting, there may be better choices. Your hero's tale may not be as interesting as her sidekick, the villain's perspective turns out to be heroic, and that throwaway character is actually more relatable.

Rosencrantz and Guildenstern are Dead is a fine example of perspective switching. It's about Hamlet from the point of view of two other characters. They also reveal a truth I agree with: the cast of *Hamlet* is a bunch of basket cases.

The main character you started with may not be the one you *need*. Be willing to change.

Where To Start?

Maybe you have a different problem–. Maybe you build a world with so much going on and you aren't sure where to start in telling the tales. You've got a potential cast of hundreds, or you have a world so detailed you could just whip up someone new to tell your stories. Where do you start?

If you have to evaluate a current main character for a demotion, or a side character for a promotion, I find these are good rules:

1) A good main character or characters can tell enough of the story from their viewpoint). They don't have to see everything, but enough to tell the story you want to tell.

2) A good main character knows enough for the audience to understand what's going on via their perspective. It doesn't have to be everything or even the majority of things. Jut enough.

3) A good main character is relatable for the audience. They don't have to be like the audience, just someone the audience "gets." A good writer can make characters that are vastly different than the target audience but are still characters people understand.

4) You can, of course, have several main characters to tell the whole tale – but they will need to be "tied together" somehow, either by narrative or with references, to work for your audience.

Use this checklist to evaluate your main character or characters for the story you're telling. You just might be surprised at who can tell your tale and how – and who can't.

More Character Than World

If you're the kind of person who created many characters before the setting (as happens the majority of the time), then the checklist above is quite important. There's a good chance the world you made has gotten far more complex and populous and your story might not be best served by the initial perspective.

However, an additional danger you face is that your world may not be fleshed out enough – just enough to tell the tale of your cast. You've got enough to tell their story, but their story is all that's going on; the rest of the setting is just a cardboard cutout, a Potemkin universe.

This happens a lot, as I'm sure we're all aware. There's a story, there's a main character, but it's happening within a peculiarly dead setting, the story equivalent of on-rails video games. It may even be a decent or a good story, but it really doesn't involve much worldbuilding and thus seems lifeless.

I find a great way to avoid this is a simple rule:

Do you know your world well enough that, if you couldn't use any of your main characters to tell your tales, you have enough characters or potential characters to tell them anyway?

These characters may not be the ones you wanted, or they may not tell the tale you way you wanted. If it can be told, then you're good. This is a good measure of the world's completeness, especially if you started with specific main characters in mind.

If you don't have these kinds of characters? More worldbuilding is in order.

We All Want To Be Someone

When you tell your tales, sit down and make sure you've got the right perspective or perspectives. You build a huge world and you want to make it work, make people experience it.

If you can't find the right characters, well, create some more! After all, if you build a good setting, it can produce even more ways to tell the tale there.

Characters: Goals, Methods, And Results

Stories, games, and all fictions are about characters, and what they do and why. They may not be like us; we may not like them; but it's all about them. We're watching people do stuff to get results, though we may put it in more colorful ways than "stuff."

Goals, methods of reaching them, and results are everything a story is about. In the end, you've got to save the prince so you can throw the one ring into the fiery pit of the starship engine to bypass the alien invaders before your ninja rival does. No goals, no methods, no results, no story, no interest.

Therefore, your world has to include characters that have believable goals, ways of achieving them, and results.

Which is obvious.

And, as you've heard me say many times, and doubtlessly will again, obvious is the problem. Goals and pursuing them are often quite complicated.

Goal!

First you have to know your character's goals to write them, code them, or however else you draw people into the world.

Character goals are important as they're why characters do things, and why people experiencing your world care. Admittedly, these goals may not be interesting, or noble, or even morally acceptable. But people do things for reasons, and that's what gets our interest, and why your world's characters need goals.

However, the devil is in the detail and Satan's in the small things. Your stories start with goals held by the characters you're telling the story about. To know your characters and their goals, you need to know the world they exist in.

Characters are who they are for *reasons*. Their background sets attitudes, expectations, and knowledge. They set the situations they act in and are motivated by. Their background, in short, defines their goals.

The goals your characters have, and the reason readers or players care, come from the world you've built. You have to ask where the character's goals came from.

- What is it in the character's background that led them to set these goals? What is their culture, their history, their experience?
- Was this "goal-setting" something that was traumatic, emotional, intellectual, or what? What impact has it had on the character? Something learned painfully versus something learned in abstract produces different kinds of goal-setting.
- Did the character even have any control over these experiences?
- How have these goals evolved and changed over time and why?

Characters go and pursue goals. These goals are born of the world. Knowing the world lets you know the characters and their goals – even if they're kind of weird, bizarre, or immoral.

However then characters try to reach their goals, and that means we have to consider . . .

Self Knowledge
Secondly, you need to know how much the characters know about themselves.

Think of how you have may have done things for reasons you only later understood. Have you surprised yourself at a motivation, or questioned your own principles? How many times did you set out to achieve a goal only to discover it wasn't what you wanted? Maybe it was your understanding of said goal kept you from achieving it. Or were you really trying to achieve one thing unconsciously while doing another?

You have to figure out how well your characters know themselves in order to write how they pursue goals. They may screw it up, but that's part of them being characters.

How much they do – or don't – know about themselves is going to affect your tale. A confused, messed-up character easily pursuing goals they're totally clear on is just not believable. An arrogant character whose ego seems to disappear when he plans The Great Main Quest Plot is going to seem wrong and poorly written.

Do characters understand what they do? Do they know what motivates them? Do they understand their own psychology? The more they understand themselves, the more they can meet their goals. The less they know, the more they may behave inappropriately, erratically, or just plain stupidly.

Just because they have goals in their mind doesn't mean they understand their own mind.

This is a tricky area of worldbuilding. You, a flawed person who doesn't always know themselves, has to know characters in the same boat better than they do. This may be educational, but it's also a pain.

However, when you can bring this level of knowledge to your characters, your setting and your writing of it will be all the richer – and more something that draws people in.

234 | Steven Savage

The Methods Of Madness And Gladness

Now that you've got character goals, how are they going to achieve them, - if, that is, they actually understand them. So now you figure out how they actually pursue their goals, or what abilities and skills they bring to screw their lives up by pursuing the wrong ones.

Characters actually have to bring abilities and plans to bear on what they want to do. At this point you suddenly have to answer a lot of questions – but, you hopefully already have the answers due to your worldbuilding.

- Do they actually have the ability to do what they want to do?
- If not, how do they get said abilities (time for a training montage)?
- Can they actually grow enough to achieve said goals?
- Do they even understand what they're capable of?
- Can they rally other people and resources to help them?

In almost any situation, no one is ready to meet their goals and solve problems right away. If they are, it's not exactly much of a tale. Forgetting this can lead to some rather inappropriately extended stories or games where everyone wonders why no one hauled off and killed the Dark Lord Azgarel in the first twenty minutes because they were so competent. It should take time to reach their goals.

This, of course, assumes the character can ever meet their goals. Perhaps your tale will be about failure, and you won't know that until you get to assess the character.

Impact

Finally, when it comes to characters pursuing their goals, rallying their abilities and connections, and in general doing something, we have to ask what the impact of their actions is.

Characters pursue goals, take action, and produce results. You, as the person that manifests the world as story, have to determine what results occur from those actions in pursuit of a goal. When you do that, I suggest you look back on your own experiences of doing things and how your actions turned out.

The answer? Usually not quite like you expected. We all have stories of not quite getting what we want, of unintended consequences and inappropriate successes. And of hideous failure, but that's a given.

When your characters take action you have to ask what happens from those actions. Real life is messy, and a good story doesn't always make things nice and clean. Not one that's believable at any rate.

Consider:

- Did the characters really do what they wanted to get to their goals, or did they fall short?
- Did they know they got what they wanted?
- What side effects were caused by their actions? Unintentional effects and collateral damage are always possible and not always visible (and can mean more story to tell).
- How do they feel about what they achieved – or didn't?
- How do they adjust or change?

Every action has its impact – including on the person taking action.

After awhile I find thinking about this helps you see the ever-changing nature of your setting. Well-created characters take action, use that feedback, and respond. Actions rarely have surgically precise results.

It can get messy. Then again, that's the fun in making worlds and writing about them.

Change Is In The Cards

In the end, each character who sets on a quest, each hero or heroine rallying their skills, changes your world and themselves. They set out, they act, they try to achieve. Not everything is what people want, not everything is always apply, but the world keeps turning. That's your tale, your story, your game.

And of course, the actions your characters take affect the world, and the goals and abilities of other characters.

The Stakes

Having discussed character goals, actions, and results, let's talk about the stakes characters fight for your world.

What Are We Fighting For?

Characters set out with certain goals and are trying to achieve those goals. They are, in short, fighting for something, even if we wouldn't think of it as a traditional conflict. Getting that coffee made in the morning is its own little battle, after all.

Readers and players are drawn into the goals because the world is believable, the characters well written, and the gameplay compelling. When the stakes are well-realized they both draw the into the world and enhance the experience. When stakes become our stakes, the goals our goals, the risk our risk, we're truly involved – and the world we experience is truly alive.

If you've ever dodged in real life while playing an FPS or gotten angry at a fictional character, you know how compelling a world and its realization in fiction or media can be. The stakes are real.

This is why readers love things with visceral elements. Even the worst film or story can make them sympathize with someone stuck in a situation we relate to. They get humiliation or pain. This is one reason authors and worldbuilders resort to blood, violence, sex, and fear too often: they're visceral and have that chance to draw you in.

As you may guess, the stakes are part of your world. They're what gives us a tale, what makes characters believable, and what gives us a gut-punch realization of "what's going on."

Well, We Are Fighting For It, Right?

The things that occur in your world, the challenges and risks, are born of your setting just like the characters who deal with them. They are part of the weather or the culture that you've created. What's going on, what's at risk, is part of your world.

Well, it is if you do it right.

Action-reaction, results, and risks are all part of good worldbuilding. You need to know what happens, what goes wrong, and what results occur when things are done or aren't done. When you know how things "work," then you can understand the stakes of what's going on, how the characters feel about them, and thus engage the audience. If your world isn't properly defined it becomes unbelievable, there's less visceral appeal, and suspension of disbelief gives up and goes to get a coffee.

Ever read a story where the goals seemed lame, the risks trite or poorly-created, and the sense of what people are trying to do didn't hold up? Or you'd seen it all before and felt like someone had brought in a Risky Stakes transplant from another story? The world wasn't well designed, so the risks had no meaning. The world wasn't well designed, the stakes had no meaning, the characters had no meaning, and you were just there watching a pile of stuff.

You get the idea.

How you build your world sets the stakes for characters. Now that may seem obvious, but you might forget how much your world tells you. It's easy to just throw some risks into the world to get the story going – forgetting you've designed enough to tell you what's going on. We stop building the world and start just throwing stuff into it.

Overdone Stakes

(Yes, that is a lame joke preserved from the original column.)

One problem in worldbuilding is that after we start writing our world we need to keep people's interest, so we raise the stakes ridiculously. You're probably especially aware of it from bad media and some games, where the villain apparently has a magical backside that holds plot devices, or suddenly the enemies are a lot tougher for no good reason. It's just there to ramp up difficulty and hopefully hold your attention.

This "ramp up" is often a natural result of increased competency on the part of the protagonists. As noted before, characters growing and applying themselves towards a goal is part of any tale, and thus world. It is entirely too easy to jack up up the difficulty level, as it were, to keep things going.

This is a risk because you throw out the laws of your world just to keep people's attention. Now you might be able to keep it within setting constraints, but based on many things I've seen . . . I wouldn't take the risk.

Now the answer to this is "just build a good world", but there are traps we often fall into. So to help you out, let me note a few common ways of raising the stakes that we can do without:

• **The End Of The World As We Know It – And I'm Annoyed.** Turning things into world-threatening crises when they weren't and cannot be explained may keep attention but is really obvious and worldbreaking.
• **The War Of Heaven And Hell And Good Taste.** Sometimes stories wander into supernatural territory, and next thing you know everyday life is a theological smackdown. That's good if that's your intent, but trying to get metaphysical just to keep interest can be quite lame. You can also have the stakes raise to such ridiculous levels with pasted-on-morals that

it might as well be a kind of Potemkin Apocalypse.

• **The Last Best Extremely Contrived Hope.** Another way people jack up the odds is creating a chosen one who's the only person that can save things. This is pretty much the classic Idiot Plot or Planet of the Morons. And it's unbelievable, worldbreaking, and annoying because it stands out (and it's over done).

• **The Destiny March Of History.** Suddenly, characters discover destiny, legacy, or something else that makes their struggles More Important. Meanwhile, the audience doesn't buy it.

• **The Sudden Ramp-Up.** Suddenly things are tougher . . . because. Basically you ramp up the stakes because you want the story to be exciting, or you run out of ideas. It's obvious when you do that.

Don't jack up the stakes inappropriately. Don't rip your world apart to wedge a piece of extra excitement in. It'll break your system. And sure, some creators get away with it, but some don't.

Do you want to take the risk? Are your stakes worth it?

No, they're not. Build a good world. If anything, just find the most exciting parts of it to tell.

In Closing

Know the stakes people are fighting for and what they're trying to do. Understand the results but let them be part of your setting. Otherwise you risk mapping tropes or easy-outs to keep interest, and people will know.

Onward To Your Own Worlds

Thus we come to the end of the book. I hope it's helped you think, helped you hope, and helped you become a better worldbuilder.

I also hope you've disagreed with me a few times because otherwise one of us is doing something wrong. Worldbuilding is far from being a science, and disagreement is a sign we're thinking.

So now, here at the end, I can but wish you well and hope your own worldbuilding efforts pay off. May you thrill, intrigue, interest, enrapture, and enrich people.

Good luck in your voyage to worlds yet unseen! I look forward to seeing them – and I'll see you again in Book 2.

- Steven Savage
June 15th, 2016

Appendices

Appendix A: Recording Your World

So you want to build a nice detailed setting and keep an archive on it. You are ready to keep a record of everything so you review and expand your work. You're ready to dive into this and put your world to pen, keyboard, map, and file.

This raises the question of just *how* you record everything.

If you've ever visited a fan wiki or purchased one of those "world of . . ." books that attempts to distill a novel or series of novels into a record of that universe, you know there is a lot of data to record a world. It can be a little daunting when you want to create your setting in detail and you realize you're creating one of those *giant* guides. And then some.

And write your world.

And you have to save it for reference.

So what's the best way to do it?

Well, that's actually several questions. So let's get to them to see what works for you.

The Format

The first question is, just how are you going to store all of this information? There are a wealth of opportunities out there from text files to full wikis which is really great until you have to actually make a choice. Then it gets kind of confusing.

Really, the best option is to find what works for you. Here's the usual things I see:

Text Files/RTF files

Your plain text file from Notepad or TextEdit or whatever is a great way to record information. I've used this method ever since I began writing extensively on a computer, and I still do as I write this. This book itself was originally composed in a text editor.

Reasons to use text/RTF files:

- Almost every computer, operating system, phone, etc. has a free editor compatible with text files (or even RTF files).
- The functionality is usually simple and clear.
- Text/RTF files are compatible with most viewing systems and you can convert them any time to another format.
- You don't rely on any specialty applications or formatting.

Reason not to use text/RTF files:

- Highly limited functionality.

Text/RTF files are also a good way to store information before you move it to another format, which I often do. Speaking of other ways to store information . . .

Word Processors

Word processors give us the advantage of having, well, all the word processor tools available. Advanced search and replace, formatting, word counts, and so on. Some of them are pretty powerful to the level of "most people don't use 80% of this stuff." They're even compatible with each other to an extent, though I haven't found this very reliable.

The advantages here are:

- Far, far more extensive features than your average text editor lets you do a lot more with charts, formatting, etc.

- Better file conversion options at your fingertips – HTML, text, PDF, and so on.
- Reasonably common features and file compatibility.
- If you wanted to publish or convert this information to another format, it's already partially there.
- You can make templates to make your life easier.

The disadvantages are:

- Compatibility issues. That has changed over the years, but I find they're still a problem.
- May not need all the features for the limits.
- Not lightweight.

For me, word processors are sort of the last line when I store information, unless I'm specifically leveraging their functions. I format my work in word processors as a last step.

Wikis And Content Systems
This requires a little work on your part, be it setting up the wiki or installing the actual software. Wikis are powerful for the obvious reason that they let you store, search, and link everything. As I mentioned earlier, a fan wiki is often an example of the sheer power of recording world information in a wiki.

Why go with a Content Management System?

- Powerful editing and formatting tools.
- Ability to link and connect your information.
- Though it may take some technical knowledge, there are many options.
- In a few cases you can probably build a fan or public wiki with a quick upload/conversion.
- You learn how to set one up.

248 | Steven Savage

Why not?

- You need some knowledge to use them.
- You're dependent on another technology that often lacks support.
- It may be way more than you need.
- You have to get access to the wiki or set it up on your system.
- Exporting it to other formats may be troublesome.

Other Writing Tools

Any aspiring writer can find a legion of other writing tools to help you craft your next tale. If you subscribe to any magazines, visit any writer website, and so on you're probably more than familiar with them due to all the ads you see. I'm not too hot on these as they seem specialized, work only certain ways, and frankly are kind of pricey. I don't like the idea of paying money to think like someone else. However:

Why get these writing tools:

- They are specialized for specific needs.
- Some have interesting or unusual tools you can't find anywhere else.

Why not?

- File formats may not be compatible with other applications.
- You have to think like the person who created the software.
- Cost – you have to pay for them and they have a specialized use. Buying an office suite is at least going to be usable elsewhere.

So as you may guess, I'm not up on these writing tools. Only use specialist tools if you need them, and always be sure you can export, save, or otherwise get the data into another format.

Fusion Solution
Finally, you may just use a fusion solution and use several tools. This is my approach, where I usually do all my basics in a text editor and then use fancier stuff as needed.

Advantages:

- A best-of-all-worlds solution.
- You have sets of different historical documents giving you a history and the ability to revert.

Disadvantages:

- A problem in the chain can disrupt you.
- You need to be sure you're not overly dependent on one solution.

So there's your options as I see them. Once you pick one (or more), the next question becomes "just what do I record from my world and how do I do it?"

How Do I Record My World?
So you've picked a method – or multiple methods – to record your world's information What exactly are you going to store in the first place?

Now, if you've decided to use some specialized software it may limit and/or enable certain ways of recording information. I'm going to assume you've elected a more freeform solution. That freeform solution, however, means you have to choose what to write down/type up/design to track all of this stuff.

I've found the best way to do this is to do a few things:

1) Act as if what you're writing down will be read by someone else. Imagine you have an inheritor, a partner, a friend, or a legion of loyal fans you want to read this. This gets you to write things down for "another," thinking what is vital to get your point across.

2) Look at other books and wikis and resources about worlds. Usually you can see some useful patterns, levels of details, and concepts you can adapt quickly.

3) Look at resources that deal with world information like roleplaying games, atlases, and so forth to see what information is seen as relevant.

4) Draw up some basic templates for things you need to record like characters, nations, and so on.

5) Wing it and start since you can always modify it later.

You are never going to design the perfect archive for your great worldbuilding because you'll only learn what you need by doing it. You can give yourself a pretty good start by seeing how others do it, get some basic forms, and go for it.

Myself, I was most influenced by roleplaying games, writer's groups (who often involved character profiles following some common patterns), and fan resource books. Some of it's worked for me for years, and some of course, changed.

In the end, I think of #1 as the most important rule of all. Accessibility is important to any record of worldbuilding, and keeping the right perspective ensures that what you design and record is something you can use, since you're thinking of it being used by others. That acts as a good guide to doing this right and a way to know when you're doing it wrong.

Moving Forward

Good luck with recording your world. In fact, as a final suggestion, share what you learn with others. Share your preferred methods, templates, and ideas. You'll help others and maybe learn a few things.

A bit like I have.

Appendix B: Worldbuilding And Language

When I first wrote the sections on race and species you read earlier, my friend Blaze at Trilobyte Studios (located at **www.trilobytestudios.com**) disagreed with my initial conclusions. Originally I felt we should give in on race versus species and use the term "race" as that was often used for species. He felt that in our craft we should be careful on proper language – and in time I realized he was right, which you can see in the above section on race and species.

Worldbuilding is a form of craftsmanship, and the language we use is important. So I'd like to take a moment here in this Appendix to address the challenges and issues of language and worldbuilding for your consideration.

The Challenge Of Worldbuilding And Language

Language is extremely important when discussing worldbuilding. Yes, that's obvious, but Blaze made me think about how important it is to have standards in language. Casual terminology and isn't the right set of terms to use when discussing worldbuilding.

Consider all the challenges facing worldbuilders when it comes to even talking about the craft:

- First there is the language of our creation itself, of basic terms. What is magic or technology, species or race, sentient and not? We must be specific to know what we are talking about.
- Specific issues such as economics or technology require specific language. Without it we can neither discuss nor research it, let alone write or explain it.
- Cultural references require understanding of culture, meaning, and history, which in turn requires specific language.

- Religious, theological, and mystical terms may be used in worldbuilding; these terms may not be understood by everyone, or they may have a lot of misunderstanding, or ambiguity. Clarity of language is important for both worldbuilding and simply for helping an audience understand when they experience your world.
- We may outright invent language or terms for our worlds, which, if we're not careful, may not be easy to communicate with our fellow creatives.

Looking at the issues of language, it almost makes you amazed anyone can craft a coherent setting, and yet we do. Many of us build unforgettable vistas that are just behind our eyes or pixels on a screen. It's all done with words.

Thus I think we worldbuilders should take the time to weigh our language carefully. What words do we use? What is appropriate? What is not appropriate/ What communicates best?

We might not even agree on everything, but we can at least hone our knowledge, our vocabulary, and our use of words to make sure we're using them right.

In fact, this leads me to a most interesting question – one that has no answer yet – but one we should consider.

A More Unified Language Of Worldbuilding?

Blaze also made me wonder if perhaps we worldbuilders should take some effort, be it debate or book or web page, to come up with a kind of "language guide" to worldbuilding. Something that worldbuilders could pick up and get the best idea of how to use words, communicate, and employ language in creation, documentation, and communication of our world.

Just consider this:

- Imagine best words to refer to particular things (like, say, race and species) that are both correct and relevant.
- Proper terminology for important scientific, religious, and political terms. Perhaps a top 100.
- Proper terms for documentation, storage, and methods that we'll use to build our worlds.
- Language traps. Words people might get wrong.
- Terms around the world that may be useful to know (or steal).

Maybe we worldbuilders should take a stab at finding a way to codify our passion with useful terminology.

We might even invent some new, needed words.

Most Certainly Not In Closing

So I leave this open to you, dear reader. What do you think? Should we worldbuilders work to hone our language and terminology a bit more? Could we?

I don't have an answer. But maybe some of us can find one together.

Appendix C: Worldbuilding And The Benefits

Previously I've discuss the benefits of worldbuilding in real life, such as improving record keeping and the like. Truth be told, there are other benefits than the more technical and procedural skills, ones that go far beyond writing. Things that make you a better, smarter, person.

This may sound a little weird. You may truly enjoy that giant mecha slam-bang universe you created, but you hardly think transforming robots really is going to make a difference in who you are or how you see things. However, it will – writers and worldbuilders find that the act of creation changes them.

I've seen this myself. Having done worldbuilding myself (in complete and far more unfinished projects), and having analyzed it, it's changed me. Having talked to writers and artists, I've been amazed how the act of worldbuilding actually improves people as people.

So if you're aware of it, then you can appreciate it, use it, and enhance it. I'm not saying everyone should sit down and create an epic sci-fi universe or fantasy epic, but I'm noting that it does more than you may think.

Here's where it helps.

Worldbuilding Gives You A Better Grasp Of Cause And Effect

Ever wonder just why people make stupid decisions? Ever look at a politician discussing a plan that seemed to be created by an insane person? Ever wonder if these people actually understood cause and effect?

Well they don't or they're ignoring it.

Cause and effect are core to good planning, good results, and in a way are part of being human. We're able to evaluate where we want to go and what we want, determine what caused what, and use it. Every building you walk by, every criminal case solved, every recipe cooked – they all involve cause and effect.

And a lot of really, really stupid, deadly stuff is the result of people deciding cause and effect need a time out from each other.

When you do worldbuilding you are hip-deep in cause and effect. You think about what happens when something is done. You ask how things are made. You wonder "what if?"

Sure, speculating on what happens when N'gormath, High Lord of Necromancy escapes the Pit of Unsundering and is turned loose on Mogwarth seems trite, but it's still contemplating cause and effect. Be it zombies or food processing, thinking about what happens when "X" happens is thinking about how results come about.

A good sense of cause-and-effect is a kind of skill, a skill that gets burned into your bones and into your mind. It's almost like Martial Arts, and people who get cause and effect instinctively are amazing planners, thinkers, and achievers.

Worldbuilding, being all about cause and effect, is burning that experience into your soul. Every question, every elaborate outline is making you better at determining the results of actions. Every time you build some complex part of your setting (even if no one sees it), you grasp mechanical connections and subtle principles.

This helps you in life, as a person – and sets you above quite a few politicians and pundits.

Worldbuilding Teaches Perspective-Shifting

Ever wonder why some people seem trapped in their own heads (except you, you're right most of the time)? Ever wonder why some people just can't see things through other people's eyes even when said people aren't lacking empathy or understanding? How is it they can't see outside their own minds?

They don't know how to shift perspectives. Good worldbuilding actually teaches you to shift perspectives. It's one way to get better at being in other people's shoes.

When you've got a huge world running and you're thinking about who did what, you have to "jump" between the minds of your characters. When your world is in gear and you're coding behavior for a game or playing an NPC or writing a scene, you have to shift perspectives. It's like a juggling act and it's in your own head. Sometimes when you build a world or create adventures in it you're not just an author or a coder, you're a group or a team or a country.

The old story about walking a mile in another person's shoes? Good worldbuilders have more pairs of shoes than an outlet store and they run marathons in them.

This is an extremely valuable ability to develop for many reasons:

- It allows you to see things from different viewpoints. Imagine being able to be in the shoes of a friend or a loved one or a stranger and just what you can learn.
- It makes a difficult skill a habit so you can access it easier.
- It keeps you from getting full of yourself as you literally are used to getting outside of your head.
- It teaches you how people see things.

Most of us would love to see more of those above abilities. When you're a worldbuilder, there's one more person in the real world who can see through the eyes of another.

You Learn To Ask Questions

Ever wonder about people who seemed incurious? Who didn't seem to be curious, to ask questions, to try and delve deep into things. Ever seen them screw up and have to note "uh, if you'd explored this a bit more . . ."

You probably have.

Worldbuilding is all about learning to ask questions, from "how would this person react?" to "what if I could use magic to fling a sun through hyperspace at a galaxy-sized angry god?" Worldbuilding gets you into the question-asking modem that is so vital to doing more.

This ties into the understanding of cause and effect that people develop in good worldbuilding, and usually a good sense of cause and effect comes from question-asking. At the same time, it's a good separate skill as it just keeps you asking "why?" and "what?"

This really means worldbuilding helps you develop a good, even fun, sense of inquiry. This assists you in many areas of your life, developing that curiosity to ask questions people didn't even think need to be asked. It's broadening.

Asking questions can lead to actual answers.

But How Do You Use This?

So, yes, I think worldbuilding makes us better people. How do you actually put it to use?

The answers is actually something I say all the time. *Be aware of it.*

Be aware of the things you're learning, and the skills and abilities you're building. Be aware that you're gaining something from all of this that goes beyond the game or the book or the comic. Acknowledge it, respect it, and bring it to the fore.

To give you a personal example, in one of my many unfinished projects I was doing some worldbuilding, and from it found that some of my cause-and-effect analysis was spot on (as it was a real world story). Taking that cue, I realized what I'd learned and worked to hone that analysis to be more useful so I could better understand some technical and cultural trends.

And no, I'm not going into detail because I feel a bit silly of what I missed.

So, be aware, be proud, and put this to use. Every day, every time you world build, you're really improving yourself.

Plus you're creating amazing, cool, interesting, fun, scary, things. It's a double win.

About The Author

Steven Savage is a lifetime geek. Starting with a childhood interest in science, science fiction and computers, to an IT career that started in his twenties, he's never stopped being an unrepentant geek.

His goal is to use his experiences and interests to help people in their careers and lives; especially his fellow geeks, fans, and otaku. To that end he writes books on pretty much whatever interests him that he thinks will help people, blogs, speaks at conventions, and more.

You can contact Steve at his website **www.StevenSavage.com**.

You can find his books at **www.InformoTron.com**.

You can find his creative tools and generators at
www.SeventhSanctum.com.

Made in the USA
Lexington, KY
29 October 2016